Little Seed Publishing
Laguna Beach, CA

Pre-press Management by New Caledonian Press
Text Design: Angie Kimbro

Cover Design and Illustrations: K-Squared Designs, LLC, www.k2ds.com

Publisher intends this material for entertainment and no legal, medical or other professional advice is implied or expressed. If the purchaser cannot abide by this statement, please return the book for a full refund.

Acknowledgement is made for permission to quote copyrighted materials.

Publisher acknowledges that certain chapters were originally published in similar or identical form in other *Wake Up...Live the Life You Love* books and reprinted by permission of Little Seed Publishing, with all rights reserved.

For information, contact Little Seed Publishing's operations office at Global Partnership: P.O. Box 894, Murray, KY 42071, or phone 270-753-5225 (CST).

Distributed by Global Partnership, LLC
P.O. Box 894
Murray, KY 42071

Library of Congress Cataloguing in Publication Data
Wake Up...Live the Life You Love: Living In The Now
ISBN-13: 978-1-933063-18-8

$14.95 USA $14.95 Canada

Other books by Steven E, and Lee Beard

Wake Up…Live the Life You Love:
…*First Edition*
…*Second Edition*
…*Inspirational How-to Stories*
…*In Beauty*
…*Living on Purpose*
…*Finding Your Life's Passion*
…*Purpose, Passion, Abundance*
…*Finding Personal Freedom*
…*Seizing Your Success*
…*Giving Gratitude*
…*On the Enlightened Path*
…*In Spirit*
…*Finding Life's Passion*
…*Stories of Transformation*
…*A Search for Purpose*
…*Living in Abundance*
…*The Power of Team*
…*Living in Clarity*
…*Wake Up Moments*
…*Wake Up Moments of Inspiration*
…*Empowered*
…*In Service*

Wake Up…Shape Up…Live the Life You Love

WAKE UP...
LIVE THE LIFE YOU LOVE

Living In The Now

TABLE OF CONTENTS

INTRODUCTION

People destined for success can still escape their destinies.

The process is not difficult and the tragedy is common. All the elements for remarkable success may be in place, yet these folks cannot live to their fullest potential. Why not?

The secret is to live in the now. It is not enough to be alive; we must live in the present moment or our hopes and dreams may never materialize.

Life teaches us lessons that can lead us forward, but some people remember only the pain of failure or the joy of success. They dwell on the pain, letting life become a series of startled jumps away from threats, real or imagined. Or, they relive happiness so often that it becomes a dependency, preventing them from experiencing new joys and even greater achievements. They live in the past.

Dreams are essential; visions of the future must be clear and compelling. People with dreams and visions are the ones who achieve things beyond their expectations. Yet, dreams can be seductive inducements which pull us into an illusory world of unrealistic possibilities. "Potential" is a beautiful jewel, but cannot quite be touched. Many people live in the future, avoiding the present—the one place where the future is constructed.

"Living in the now" means more than getting up every day to push back the curtains of possibility. It means that we realize and appreciate everything in our lives, so that life becomes more real, more precious and more rewarding. "Feel the water on your hands while you are doing dishes," says Steven E. "Feel the wind on your face. Stop to look at the faces of your children while they play; concentrate on their joy and energy. That's the now; that's what is real, and that's where life takes place."

How are you living your life "in the now?"

Have you ever dwelt on the past or longed for a dream-like future, only to be shocked into the now by someone or something? Read the lessons learned from those who woke up to the gift of the present.

Are you creating the life you love by "living in the now?" If you're not sure, read the descriptions of those who believe they are, and understand the steps to becoming one who lives in the moment.

Read the stories of those who were trapped in the past or bound by fears of the future. Read how they escaped into the now.

Finally, don't be alarmed at the distinction between the "now" and the present; in subtle ways, they are not the same thing. As you read, you will discover the important difference and, we hope, the ways in which you can make the fullest use of the time you have.

The publishers are indebted to the hard work of editors Brian Truskey and his team: Jay Dyer, Amy Wilson, Sara Andrus, Darlisha Stanfield, Caitlin Spencer, Kara McCombs and Kimberley Cottingham. We appreciate the contributions of Rita Oldham, the business manager for this project, and the staff of New Caledonian Press. We are indebted to the work of Justin and Angie Kimbro of K-Squared Designs for their presentation of these concepts in an attractive, useful form.

Our thanks, as well, to Leslie Sullivan and her associates at Lightning Source, Inc., and to Paul Bryant at CPS, who helped us through the process of making these books available throughout the world.

And, of course, we thank you. You will share the hopes and intentions of the writers and, if your dreams are realized, you will find yourself living in the now.

Let's begin the journey.

—Robert Valentine
Senior Editor

WAKE UP...
LIVE THE LIFE YOU LOVE

Living In The Now

"HOW" IS ABOUT "NOW"
Steven E

"The secret of health for both mind and body is not to mourn for the past, not to worry about the future or not to anticipate troubles, but to live in the present moment wisely and earnestly."—Buddha

The present moment is a precious gift from God. All that any of us really have is *now*. However, most of us spend our time worrying about the past or the future rather than living in the present moment.

Go With the Flow
Most people are taught that life is hard work and difficult. However, looking around at nature, we see its simplicity and flow: Birds flying effortlessly, an abundance of trees and flowers flourishing. Our universe is continually flowing and your life can join the flow.

When you want something in life, do you struggle in the process, or does it flow into your life? Life works so much better when you do not need to push and shove to materialize your desires. Of course, we need to take action when we want or need something in our lives, but we don't need to lace our actions with negative emotions. Let the doors open, and flow effortlessly through life.

When people rush around and take life so seriously, it often reflects a lack of maturity. Run from those people because life was not meant to be that serious and hard.

I have learned that if someone else can achieve something in life, I can too. Learn to go within. Spend time with yourself and love yourself. Feel good about who you are. This is not just positive thinking; it goes far deeper. Go within and pull out your negative weeds. Plant seeds that are loving and flowing, then watch the change from a life of struggle to the life you love.

Visualize Your Dreams
The most important part of visualization is to make sure you feel it. Plant the seeds and know that someday your seeds will become beautiful flowers. Just wait and let go. There is no reason to dig up the seeds you planted. Make sure you water them daily and have faith.

Practice this visualization with your relationships. See yourself with more unconditional love, joy, compassion and anything and everything your heart desires.

Write down three things you would like to manifest in your life. Carry these goals in your pocket and throughout the day. Look at your goals and concentrate. Feel them being in your life. Feel that they exist in the present moment, in the *now*. The more you observe and concentrate on your goals, the faster they will come to you.

Don't Despair
History's visionaries never worried about how change would come about. They pictured an ideal world and inspired people to share in their visions.

"When I despair, I remember that all through history the ways of truth and love have always won. There have been tyrants, and murderers, and for a time they can seem invincible, but in the end they always fall. Think of it—always."—Mahatma Gandhi.

Steven E

LETTING GO
Ben "BC" Green

M ark Twain once said, *I am an old man and have known a great many troubles, but most of them never happened.*

It's the little things that get under our skin that tend to entrap us in the ways of this world. Janis Joplin explained freedom as being just another word for having nothing left to lose. Jesus Christ said a man should leave his possessions and follow Him. The reality of this is dialectical. Previously, I thought the reference was to literal possessions, but only recently have I discovered it is the meanings we associate with them.

My daughter, Grace, gave me a Christmas ornament about a year ago. It was a figurine of a penguin wearing a scarf and holding a bowling ball—both are sliding toward the pins. It still remains on my desk as a reminder that sometimes you just have to let go. It was given to me a week early because she knew I needed it. I was totally overwhelmed. I was lost in despair and hopelessness. How did I arrive at this place? I was depressed and feeling trapped in a seemingly inescapable prison of expectancies. Depression has become one of America's biggest plagues and it is creating a population of medicated individuals who are numb to reality. I was one of those people until I woke up in response to the insight of my 12-year-old daughter.

I had no reason to feel the way I did. My life was not one of self-absorption, but rather of self-sacrifice. Perhaps you feel that you too need to satisfy those around you by sacrificing your own needs. Perhaps your values seem less important than the values of those you serve. Maybe you are a victim of your own perceptions and you feel trapped by the circumstances that define your life. For me, letting go meant redefining the constructs of my life to allow for new realities to exist in my world. It meant focusing on *being* rather than *doing*. This was the beginning of my awakening to what life was really meant to be.

I let go of false beliefs and closed the door of opportunity. I awoke to the notion that to help others, I must first fill my own cup. I had been pouring myself out without refilling. Now I realize the cup of life tastes best when it is filled until it overflows onto all those who come near.

You may be wondering what happened when I "let go" of my past judgments and concerns for the future. When I realized I could still be a husband, father and responsible citizen while being carefree at the same time, I truly began to live. I stopped depending on myself and began trusting completely in God. In finding the freedom to pursue the important things in my life, I have unleashed the artist in me, forged ahead in my life-coaching and stepped out in faith to go forward, rather than seeking the false security of standing still. I found the "I am" in myself and let go of the perceptions of what I thought I was.

How is your cup? Are you filling it only so that you may drink from it, or are you pouring it out until you feel empty and drained? Seek to continually refill it, letting it spill out to those you love and to those who need love. Holding onto the past and your old belief systems creates a world filled with false perceptions. Letting go of all we know and seeing the world through the eyes of God brings to us a freedom described in all of the most ancient of texts, but rarely understood or actualized.

I challenge you to let go of all the junk in your past that clouds your mind, weakens your heart and steals your dreams. Stop worrying about what the future may bring and live in the now. Does it mean forsaking all you are or know? No. It means letting go of what you think yesterday and tomorrow have in store. Instead, live today and savor the flavor of every experience as it happens. Take risks and follow your heart. Invest yourself in those around you. Your world will become new.

Benefits of Letting Go
My personal experience of letting go includes releasing inner resistance and inhibitions, eliminating stress and increasing energy, inspiration and creativity. My needs are met and my desires magically appear, often in unexpected ways, showing me that miracles can happen.

Words of Wisdom for the Power of Letting Go
"We must be willing to let go of the life we have planned, so as to accept the life that is waiting for us." —Joseph Campbell

"We must learn to let go, to give up, to make room for the things we have prayed for and desired." —Charles Fillmore

"Trying creates impossibilities, letting go creates what is desired."—Stalking Wolf, Apache Elder

"When I let go of what I am, I become what I might be. When I let go of what I have, I receive what I need."—The Tao Te Ching

Have you ever struggled to find work or love, only to receive them after you have finally given up? This is the paradox of letting go in order to achieve. Letting go is God's law. Are you ready to let go and receive what you seek now?

Ben "BC" Green

LIVING LIFE FROM THE END
Christine M. Prevete, Mh.D.

I've got a secret to tell. I consider it a secret because nobody ever told me. I discovered it purely by experience and no one ever talks about it. This secret is a key that opens the door to a truly joyful life filled with excitement, pleasure, vitality and empowerment.

The good news is that we all have this key. The key is called willingness: the ability to think of your life from the end. Yes, that's right; I said "the end." I know this may sound absurd, and you might be tempted to stop reading right here. After all, when was the last time you encountered anyone who considered the end of his life with optimism? Do you know anyone willing to think of the subject? I assure you, this is a powerfully liberating suggestion that will jump-start your day, every day. If spending your day full of passion and creativity sounds intriguing, stick with me.

I was forced to accept the truth of "the end" when my mother passed from her physical life at a young age. Through trying to "save" her from a physical illness and through enduring her departure, the most incredible secret about life bloomed right before my eyes. Being with her at her passing was further confirmation for me that we continue to live on and there really is no "end," but that is a story for another time. There is an end to this physical experience we call life. The story we are living does have a conclusion and the truth is that the end *could* be today. What if it were? It is this possibility of the end that can and *should* inspire us to wake up!

Why would I suggest such a commonly avoided thought for inspiration, because it is eye-opening, liberating and inspirational. How many people do you know who are living their lives exactly as they desire? How many people do you meet who are eager to share with you all the good news in their lives? Have you found typical conversations to be filled with complaints of stress, overload or what's wrong in the world? Our lives are temporary and short-lived. Must they always be filled with endless days of obligation and duty with only pockets of pleasure? Are those pockets of pleasure really and truly pleasure, or are they social obligations?

Let me say again that life is temporary. There is no getting around it. So what can you do with this fact? I suggest not waiting until the last minute to panic. I sincerely hope this story, rather than your own crisis, will be your wake up call. I have felt that panic and it is the worst feeling in the world. I have lived through the torture of looking at my mother's empty room and saying, "That's it? She's done? There's nothing else?" The revelation of life ending quickly led to a huge, wake up for me.

That day was the end of my mother's physical existence, but it felt like the beginning of mine—it was my wake up call. I decided it was time to be happy and to do what I love. It was time to be honest about what brings me joy and stop the drudgery of doing only what I "should" do. When I am called from my physical life, I want to look back at where I've been and say, "Yes, all feels complete. I have created and I have loved. I have inquired and I have learned. Through my five senses, I have learned the ways to develop my inner senses." I want to complete the journey knowing my life's purpose was fulfilled.

My mission of living a pleasing life began by imagining I had only six months left to live. I would frequently ask myself, "If I had only six months left here on earth, what would I choose?" With a sincere mindset of answering this question consistently, my life has dramatically changed for the better. I left the corporate track and pursued a path of passion. I became self-employed, which had been my dream. I found myself expressing love toward my husband and children by being present more. I immersed myself in enjoying people and educating myself on subjects I adored.

The exercise of asking myself this question has changed over the years. I have made it from "six months" all the way to "this moment." The question no longer even needs to be asked because it is now a given. I have gone from a corporate, indoor position to writing this story at the beach on a beautiful day while my children play at my feet. My quest for education led to a degree in metaphysics. I understand what being in service truly means, and it has nothing to do with being a "people pleaser."

What has evolved is an appreciation of life with each new day. My morning prayer is to live for today by experiencing life exactly as I "will" instead of as I "should." My expression toward others is as mindful as possible as I try to improve and offer support and love for all. Each day is completed by gratefully "dying" into sleep. I reflect back on the day, celebrate my successes, try to learn from the unsuccessful and equally give thanks for the awareness of it all.

So the secret key to that spark in my eye is now in yours as well. It's the willingness to understand that you can choose. You can hear the baby crying and wish it would stop, or you can hear the baby's call to be cradled in your loving arms and thank God you can hear his voice. You can complain about that job you have to do, or you can give thanks for the skills that enable you to be self-sufficient and supplied. You can be annoyed by the attitudes of others, or you can show up in the world with the prayer in your heart, "How may I serve?" The blessing is that you can choose.

When I was growing up, one of my favorite movies was *It's a Wonderful Life*. When video tapes were available, it was the first movie my mom bought me. I thought I loved the movie because I loved Jimmy Stewart and the message about angels getting their wings. But now I know it was even more than that. It inspired me to remember what my soul knew all along: It really is a wonderful life, if we can just be conscious enough to realize it—*NOW*.

Christine M. Prevete, Mh.D.

LIVING IN THE HERE AND NOW
Aila Accad, R.N.

I have read and heard many gurus talk about "being here," "living in the now" and "being present in the moment." However, not one of those books or speakers told me how to do it. It reminds me of when I was a senior in nursing school. My instructor said, "You have to know yourself before you can really connect with and know your patients." I said, "Okay, how do I do that?" She had no answer.

Many people seem to come to awareness spontaneously and cannot really tell you how they did it. They can just say you need to be present, aware, and stop living in the past or the future. That's great, but how?

If you are like a lot of my clients and me, you're a seeker of truth and a lifelong learner who doesn't understand why—after all the training and reading you've done—you are not able to find peace or happiness. You feel guilty, defective and alone in this process.

Spontaneous enlightenment was not my experience. I found a slow, steady route to living in the now. If you don't have a Bodhi tree, park bench or near-death experience to catapult you into the now, maybe my discoveries on the path will support you in finding your way to the here and now, knowing you are not alone.

Living in the Then and When
For much of my life I lived in what happened back then and dreamed about when the happiness payoff would come in the future for all the hard work I was doing now. As a first-born child, I lived to please my parents and worked hard at it. My mother was not easily pleased. I became a nurse to please her, married the man she approved of and went through a grueling infertility process to attempt to give her grandchildren.

Eventually, we adopted a beautiful baby boy and I thought I had found the answer to my life's meaning and purpose. That was short-lived in the daily effort to be the perfect parent. I became the ultimate co-dependent, nurturing parent for everyone who needed me. I thought that was my purpose.

I made taking care of others and taking responsibility for everything an art form. Energetically, I drew on some cache of strength that never seemed to run out, until my birthday, October 6, 1987, when I crashed. I pulled the covers over my head and prayed to disappear for three months. I wasn't suicidal, just exhausted. I wanted to start over with a clean slate.

My bedridden mother had come to live with us after my father died the previous August. I handled the funeral arrangements and never grieved. At the same time, I was pursuing a master's degree in nursing and was managing a household, kids, husband and everything else on the list. I felt completely alone. Mom died unexpectedly on February 4, six months to the day after Dad died. I completed and defended my thesis and graduated in May of 1988.

Feeling numb, I lived in limbo for an entire year. The people I lived to please were gone. My purpose was gone and I felt like an orphan with no direction. My inner resources were exhausted and I needed help. This student was ready and the teachers appeared.

The Transition Process

Guidance
I met my first guide through a friend. JR was the perfect teacher for me. He sat still and gently guided me through the limitations of my past conditioning toward finding an abiding truth within myself. A guide is essential to mirror one's true nature and dismantle the ego conditioning that protects it. To live in the now, we must come home to our selves rather than to the image of who we grew up thinking we were. Set your intention, then wait for a guide to show up who has walked this path and knows the terrain.

Simplification

I learned to simplify my life, to be responsible for only myself, to abandon expectations of others, to delegate, and to develop a simple daily plan to take care of my physical, emotional and spiritual needs. I learned to let go of the emotional and physical baggage I was carrying in order to free up energy and time to be in the now.

Nature Connection

Without my old, familiar patterns, I became restless and edgy. I would go out and sit in the yard every half hour or so. We had a steep, sloped yard with no landscaping. With no knowledge of planting, I got a catalog and read about the growing needs and blooming times for plants.

I had a hole dug into the hillside for a tiered pond with a waterfall. Then, day by day, I added stone steps and planted trees, flowers and shrubs, one at a time, over the course of a couple of years. A beautiful year-round garden emerged.

Through this process, I became intimate with Mother Nature and my own nature. I observed how the microcosm and macrocosm of life mirrored one another. It is awesome how the natural order of nature's systematic interdependence works the same way on all levels of life. Nature captured my attention and showed me how to live in constant change and in a nurtured presence.

Meditation

My mind, with all of its questions and knowledge, was my strength and master. I learned to put it in proper alignment with my soul. It needed to become the servant rather than the leader. As the mind quieted, intuitive knowing strengthened. Choosing the next steps in the now became easier and more trusted as my mind learned to let go of needing to know and predict the future.

Curiosity

This is not the curiosity of asking questions and seeking answers, but rather the curiosity of just being interested in what is happening in this moment and seeing, hearing, and feeling experiences for the first time. Every experience is unique and happens only once. Paying attention to what is happening moment-to-moment is an adventure in awe and delight in the now.

Letting Go
Surrender control and attachment to outcomes. Release pre-judgment, expectation, ego, desire, comparison and the like. This is perhaps the hardest essential step to living in the now. You need the preceding tools to support this.

Living in the Now
Living in the now is not a destination. It is a continuous process and practice in being aware and connected to oneself and the unique adventure life presents in each lived moment. Constant gratitude, unconditional love, and freedom from fear are now's gifts.

Living in the now is like the last scene in *Indiana Jones and the Last Crusade*. Indy is about to die, the Holy Grail is across the abyss and he has no choice and nothing to lose. He steps off the cliff and the ground appears from nowhere to support his foot. He takes another step and the ground appears again until he reaches his destination.

Living in the now means enjoying each step and trusting the divine to meet your foot. With guidance and tools, you too, can learn to live in the now, even if you don't have a Bodhi tree, park bench or near death experience.

Aila Accad, R.N.

IS IT WRONG TO LIVE FOR THE MOMENT?
Sid Grosvenor

Is it wrong to live for the moment? The short answer: It depends.

If, as some do, you define "living for the moment" as being hedonistic, living with abandon and shirking your responsibilities to those you love, then the answer is a definite, "Yes." That kind of selfish living is very wrong.

We've all heard the phrase, "Stop and smell the roses" (Walter Hagen). While deep inside we know it's true, we usually pass the comment off as something we will do later, perhaps after the kids are grown, after we retire, after we get rich or after we… (Well, you can fill in the blank). Unfortunately, many people with this philosophy may never "slow down and smell the roses."

The reason: They don't know how. They were trapped by being overly focused on "making it" in the future and thus lived in the future. Then, once they made it, they had no practical experience in living in the now.

Often, these people will then revert to living in the past. They romanticized the future so they do the same with the past, talking about the good old days when they were younger, when they had responsible positions in business, were raising a family or… well, you fill in the blanks.

Why not live in the now?

Yes, we all live physically in the present until time travel is a practical consideration. We all do everyday things like shopping for groceries, washing our clothes and going to work. All those things take place in the present tense, to be sure. However, we have a choice as to just how we live in the present. You can choose to enjoy it, or fear it, or… well, you will have to be the one who fills in all the blanks.

The theme of this book is to be sure you know you have a choice and to show you some ways to actually make the choices based on the real-life experiences of the authors. I like the phrase Joyce Meyer's Ministries uses and has registered as a trademark: "Enjoying Everyday Life."®

The real key to enjoying everyday living is to notice and rejoice in the sometimes small, positive things that all around us in the now. Some people choose, without thinking, to go through the motions of living their lives and at times actually dreading or perhaps even despising their everyday lives; but that's not necessary.

In other words, you get to choose which life you want.

There's no reason to compartmentalize our enjoyment: to live only in the past or a hoped-for better future. We can live in the now and enjoy everyday life. You have the magic within you to do this.

You must guard against letting circumstances in your everyday life take you mentally to places you don't want to go. Perhaps this old vaudeville joke will remind you that you have a choice: A guy walks into a doctor's office and says, "Doctor, I broke my arm in two places." And the doctor replies, "Well, stay out of those places."

When circumstances are taking you places you know you don't want to go, you owe it to yourself to remember the punch line and to "stay out of those places."

"Sounds good," you say, "But just how do I stay away from those mental places? What's the process?"

Well, here's what works for me. If, for example, you're tempted by a rude person to go to a negative mental place, just make up a good story as to why this person was rude and forgive him instantly. If possible, respond with an understanding word and encouragement of some type, resisting the natural tendency to become defensive or hostile.

These feelings have been shown to be harmful to our physical health as well as to our mental health. The old slogan, "Courtesy is contagious," comes to mind as does the scripture, "A gentle answer turns away wrath, but a harsh word stirs up anger" (Proverbs: 15:1 NASB).

As a police officer and a divorce lawyer in former lives, I often found myself in very negative circumstances in which hostility was the common denominator. On more than one occasion, after I had handcuffed a suspect for transport to jail, I would hear, "If you take these handcuffs off me I'll kick your a—."

My stock reply proved to be just the right one to calm the prisoner and sometimes even get a chuckle out of him: "Hey, I may be just a cop, but I'm not stupid, and since I don't want you to kick my a—, I'm not taking the handcuffs off."

As a police officer, and later as an attorney, a big part of living in the now and enjoying my everyday life was seeing the good that came from what I was doing and forgiving people for being human and, when and where I could, practicing Proverbs 15:1.

After I retired from the Dallas Police Department and the active practice of law, my beloved wife Patricia and I decided to retire part-time to beautiful Lake Chapala, Mexico.

We were looking forward to a new adventure of living in a foreign country and made an offer on a home there, but then the seller abruptly changed his mind and canceled the contract. We could not believe he did this, but there it was. Fate had just slammed the door in our faces, or so we first thought.

Overcoming our disappointment, we decided to put on a happy face, knowing that things happen for a reason. Later, we were to know just why this happened. My beloved Patricia was diagnosed with leukemia a few months later and the time was not right for us to have a home in Mexico. Talk about a "wake up moment!"

We immediately began a treatment regimen of chemotherapy and later radiation therapy. The nurses were amazed at my wife's positive spirit and often remarked on how she lifted them up when normally it was their job to uplift their patients. She kept them laughing a good bit of the time.

My Patricia was the kind of person who had the ability to make close friends with someone she had never met before while standing in the check-out line at the grocery store.

She was just sure she was going to get well, but after seven months of treatment, the doctors told us to go home and enjoy the rest of our lives. Actually, we had been doing that each day, knowing that any day might be our last together.

Faced with the reality of her impending death, but also being strong in our faith, we decided we would show the world death is just a new life in a better place.

Patricia wanted to say goodbye to all her friends in this life; my job was to notify them and schedule appointments to come see her. Even as she lay dying, she had her friends laughing as they remembered all the fun times they had growing up. It was a bittersweet time.

She left peacefully in her sleep one evening in May of 2000, and woke up with the angels to live her new life in the everlasting now.

Sid Grosvenor

EMBRACE SILENCE
Dr. Wayne W. Dyer®

You live in a noisy world, constantly bombarded with loud music, sirens, construction equipment, jet airplanes, rumbling trucks, leaf blowers, lawn mowers and tree cutters. These manmade, unnatural sounds invade your senses and keep silence at bay.

In fact, you've been raised in a culture that not only eschews silence, but is terrified of it. The car radio must always be on, and any pause in conversation is a moment of embarrassment that most people quickly fill with chatter. For many, being alone in silence is pure torture.

The famous scientist Blaise Pascal observed, "All man's miseries derive from not being able to sit quietly in a room alone."

With practice, you can become aware that there's a momentary silence in the space between your thoughts. In this silent space, you'll find the peace that you crave in your daily life. You'll never know that peace if you don't have any spaces between your thoughts.

The average person is said to have 60,000 separate thoughts a day. With so many thoughts, there are almost no gaps. If you could reduce that number by half, you would open up an entire world of possibilities for yourself. For it is when you merge into the silence, and become one with it, that you reconnect to your source and know the peacefulness that some call "God." It is stated beautifully in Psalms of the Old Testament: "Be still and know that I am God." The key words are "still" and "know."

"Still" actually means "silence." Mother Teresa described silence and its relationship to God by saying, "God is the friend of silence. See how nature (trees, grass) grows in silence. We need silence to be able to touch souls." This includes your soul.

It's really the space between the notes that make the music you enjoy so much. Without the spaces, all you would have is one continuous, noisy note. Everything that's created comes out of silence. Your thoughts emerge from the nothingness of silence. Your words come out of this void. Your very essence emerged from emptiness.

All creativity requires some stillness. Your sense of inner peace depends on spending some of your life energy in silence to recharge your batteries, removing tension and anxiety, thus reacquainting you with the joy of knowing God and feeling closer to all of humanity. Silence reduces fatigue and allows you to experience your own creative juices.

The second word in the Old Testament observation, "know," refers to making your personal and conscious contact with God. To know God is to banish doubt and become independent of others' definitions and descriptions of God. Instead, you have your own personal knowing. And, as Melville reminded us so poignantly, "God's one and only voice is silence."

Dr. Wayne W. Dyer®

LIVING NOW...IN FORWARD FAST
Mark Stinson

I'm driven to accelerate the use of new medical treatments to improve quality of life for those who are suffering. People with disease, pain or disabilities can't wait. So, my daily wake-up call is to move with urgency. Learn fast. Track fast. Think fast. Respond fast. Create fast. Forward fast.

This is my focus of living in the now. That's why, right now, I want to leverage all my experience and skills in marketing, advertising, education and communications to help create "health science brands."

With the passion I have for advancing medicine, I actually gain energy from being on the move. People might tell me to slow down, or they might say I'm rushing things or that we need more time. I'm tempted to think I should rewind very slowly. Certainly there are times when I enjoy rewinding, going back to reminisce and relive an experience; but then I restart. I work hard to be creatively prepared and focused in order to reach the scientists, medical researchers, physicians, nurses, clinics and millions of patients we need to inform. So, I can't sit still—I'm living at the speed of hope.

I measure the journey not simply by speed, but by outcome; I've seen the value our health science branding approach can create in people's lives. The fact that we can touch so many people so quickly gives new meaning to medical advancement.

I've had the opportunity to work with one company that is working to change kidney dialysis and with another company which has a revolutionary device to transport kidneys for transplant. In both cases, we were working to completely change the current practice of medicine and replace older technologies. In fact, the kidney transport device was featured in *Business Week* magazine as one of the "Ten Devices Changing Medicine." With the promise of simpler routines, improved quality of life, and even better survival, we were motivated to live in fast forward—now.

One of my clients is working on cellular therapy for cardiovascular diseases and another is developing the first approved treatment for a rare disease caused by a genetic disorder in the blood. Both have been years in development, so each day we are able to help speed up the processes and get these life-changing treatments on the market can make a dramatic difference for patients and their families. So, we live in forward fast—now.

One foundation we helped brand is delivering hope to those with arthritis. Another is improving and speeding up the way hospital labs identify diseases. Both have strong clinical evidence of a better way to help people who would suffer needlessly otherwise. So, we work to communicate the news in forward fast—now.

One of our diagnostic company clients wants to get the word out that they have a better way to diagnose ovarian cancer. With another company, we need to accelerate the awareness of a treatment algorithm for sleep apnea, an often underappreciated cause of cardiovascular disease. So, living in the "now" means working in forward fast.

In your world, you can look around and see the people who take this approach. They are the ones who are
- taking charge of their personal and professional lives
- making significant choices about how they view things
- choosing their attitudes with purpose
- attracting the right talent to create teams that support their visions
- taking action to make things happen

When I meet with new clients or interview potential associates, I always ask, "Are you ready to hit the forward fast button? Because, if not, it will take too long to get where you want to be." The people who share the desire to move fast come together, work together and achieve amazing things together.

It's that chemistry of fast-minded people that has made my journey in health science branding so gratifying. I've learned so much from so many and I enjoy sharing what I've learned with others who want to make a difference.

Here's what I've found to be the definition of the chemistry of living forward fast:

C = Connect by making what you do relevant to others. You might be a "knowledge engineer" who can help take what people need and want to know, then structure it into action.

H = Honesty means being true to yourself and not trying to make your "brand" something you are not.

E = Easy is memorable. Keep it simple, but don't try to water it down. Use a chart, schematic, acronym or other tool to powerfully communicate your point.

M = Motivate your audience to action. Knowledge and attitude are only the beginning. Remember the "call to action." What do you want to happen?

This is not only the way I brand health science products; it's also my personal brand, and it's a reflection of many things—a lot of hard work, a lot of sacrifices and plenty of commitment and compassion. Most of all, heavy doses of patience, understanding and support from my wife, my children, my extended family and everyone around me.

I share this energy with you, with the hope that your own dreams and passions can move you forward fast in many powerful ways.

Mark Stinson

ACHIEVING LIFE IN "4D"
Chuck A. Reynolds

Have you ever wondered why some people achieve more success than others? The answer is they live and lead their lives differently. I find this is a significant point at which hiring managers and recruiters are looking. Globally, organizations are concerned about the leadership talent of the future. Many of our clients express this concern as they engage us to help them enhance management and team effectiveness. What we find is this: People can lead others more effectively when they lead themselves effectively. People who have a record of sustained success generally lead their own lives differently, and you can too.

You have incredible God-given strengths. If you are like most of us, you also know you are capable of much more. Like Simba's father says in *The Lion King*, "You are much more than you have become." The following points and reflection questions are designed to help you lead and live your life on purpose. Plan your future and live it now.

So how do high achievers "do" life differently? The reality is they plan out their future, then live purposefully in the now. The following is what I call the "Four D's of Personal Leadership." In a sense, we are all leaders (family, work, teams, etc.), but we can lead others better when we first lead ourselves well. If you learn and apply 4D, you will achieve more of your purpose and be an inspiration to others to do the same. Are you ready to achieve more? Here we go.

Destination
The first "D" stands for destination. I was fortunate enough to be inspired by my friend, author Brian Tracy, to set and achieve goals. His book *Maximum Achievement* remains one of my favorites. I had the opportunity to speak with him at his house in La Jolla, California, in 1995, at a dinner party with Jim Cathcart and others, and I recall him reminding us that "those without goals are forever destined to work for those with clear goals."

I have since marveled that though a person rarely, if ever, boards a plane without knowing its destination, most people awaken each Monday morning and drag themselves to work without knowing where they are going with their lives. Successful people choose where they want to arrive in their lives, rather living by accident. They achieve clarity by writing out these goal destinations.

Think about it for a moment. Waking up and living each day without clearly written goals is like riding in a bumper car with your foot on the pedal, but your hands tied behind your back instead of on the steering wheel. You'd be able to move, but with no directional control, and you'd just get bumped around a lot. Conversely, if you set clearly written goals and focus on them each day, you will be energized as you steer in your life's direction. This is a habit of high achievers that you need to acquire now!

It is ideal that you set long-term and short-term destination goals in the areas of health, family and relationships, career, spiritual life and finances. As Stan Davis suggests in his book *Future Perfect*, ask yourself this question: If you went to sleep today and woke up in three years to a life that was perfect for you in all areas, what would it look like? (Think in terms of the five categories previously listed). "*Where there is no vision, the people perish*" (Proverbs 29:18 KJV).

Decision

The second "D" stands for decision. Once achievers set their goals, they first make the decision to achieve them and then proceed to make decisions on how they will do so. Essentially, achievers start with a plan. They decide what to do and when to perform these "to do's," or as I call them, "to achieve's." Much like a road map, once you know your destination, you can easily plan your route to get from where you are to where you want to be. You must select the proper roads and directions to arrive at the desired destination. These decision steps should also be written down. It pays to plan decisive actions ahead. It wasn't raining when Noah built the ark.

Discipline

The next "D" stands for discipline. It is said that, "on the road to success, there are many tempting parking spaces." Those who have achieved much had to learn to stick to their destination-focused road map instead of taking non-productive detours.

Years ago, during a conversation with Sony Music Canada President Rick Camilleri, I learned that French-Canadian singer Celine Dion chose her destination of becoming an internationally acclaimed singer early in life. She then made the decision to learn English and practice, practice, practice, instead of spending time doing other things that would have created "success detours" while growing up in Quebec, Canada. You too will succeed when you remain disciplined enough to keep doing the things you need to do, as opposed to wasting time on non-productive tasks. The discipline to say "no" to time wasters is as much a success factor as is planning your destination.

Determination

The final "D" stands for determination. Many people set goals but never achieve them. Unknowingly, they are building a belief system that they "can't," and this becomes a success barrier.

As anyone who has completed a full marathon knows, once you start, it requires determination to finish. Any goal worth achieving will be tough at times. When you persevere to an accomplishment, you boost your internal confidence, which prepares you for even bigger goals and successes.

When you set your destination, be determined to arrive there. Just like running a marathon, take water and walking breaks when needed, but never stop until you cross the finish line. Simply put, never give up. The reward for continued perseverance and goal achievement will be an incredible burst of energy and inner confidence.

Recently I attended the funeral of a dear friend, Kate Coen. We went to grade school together 34 years ago, and she had been living with cancer the last few years. I will never forget seeing her in the hospice a few hours before she passed away, as her wonderful husband, Sean, helped their two-year-old son up onto the bed to kiss his unresponsive mom. I will never forget one of the things she said to me after I shared with her a health scare I had. She said, "Chuck, you know, for many of us, you never fully live until you know you're really dying."

May you wake up each day and really live on purpose, instead of by accident, as you practice 4D living. I wish you continued achievement as you teach others to do the same.

Some 4D questions to consider as you practice 4D living:
(Write out your answers on a piece of paper.)

Destination—Where do you want to be in three to five years? What do you want to achieve that is important to you?

Decisions—What must you do to reach your goal(s)? What steps do you need to plan to take?

Discipline—What must you do to stay on track? What time wasters must you eliminate?

Determination—What benefits will you enjoy by achieving these goals? Why are they important to you?

Chuck A. Reynolds

LIVE THE LIFE YOU WANT
Tony Whittle

In order to truly appreciate the light, they say you should experience pitch black darkness for a while. Thinking back, it was as though I was seeing the world from inside a coal cellar, where the gloom was permanent and heavy. Everyone else seemed detached, moving above and away from me. I suppose what made it worse was that everyone around me at work thought I was happy; I was anything but happy and I had to get out. I'd reached a stage in my life and my business where my deteriorating relationships with my partners meant I needed a break.

Six years earlier, I saw a media opportunity that had real potential. When I met with the two other people who were to become my business partners, I put my cards firmly on the table. "I think we can build something fast," I said. "If we get it right, in five years time, I want out after we sell and make good money!" By this, I meant enough money to do the things I really wanted. I asked if they felt the same way. I still remember them saying, "Yes, we do." What they really meant was, "Not a chance!" They said the opposite at the time.

Here I was, six years in, with several opportunities having passed me by. The three of us had indeed built something of value. With a small bank loan in 1995, we opened a tiny office in a rural English town. Within three years, we relocated our little company, The Media Vehicle, to London. It had been a roller-coaster ride, beginning our in-store advertising business inside a building in the suburbs of London. We now had a network of thousands of stores that included some of the world's largest multiple retailers. Our company had spread from the UK to Ireland, Europe, Hong Kong and Singapore. We were even developing a business on the Pacific Rim.

We created the possibility for advertisers to reach 95 percent of the country's total population while they were actually in the store. However, I was dreadfully frustrated and unhappy. The problem was that, while the business concept was sound, the standards and values we started with gradually eroded. What was once open enterprise had become the opposite. We employed only keen and enthusiastic young-sters, with no experience, but plenty of energy and fire. Instead of feed-ing and nurturing those qualities, we turned our attention away from their futures and toward the bottom line.

We had already turned down the advances of a large organization that approached us with the mention of a buy-out, which would have easily met my five-year goal. My partners voted against me and I had to sim-ply turn the investors away. I was flabbergasted. When I asked for their reasons, both claimed we should "Move on alone in order to go for the big money," though the offer on the table was more than $20,000,000!

This was my moment of revelation. In desperation, I asked both part-ners a question that was to prove pivotal. I didn't realize it then, but it was a difficult question for anyone to answer. It was to be a key to the rest of my life and the secret of living the way I wanted in the future.

I asked both partners individually and together the following question:

"How much is enough for you?"
In our collective greed and growing arrogance, we appeared to be saying all we wanted or needed was that deal. I had let myself believe they would be as content as I to sell and get out. I had been naïve and ideal-istic. Now my soft approach to business was being punished. I then faced a six-month period of disbelief. How could I have been so simple-minded, thinking people would do what they said? In my mid-40s, I actually thought one could be open and honest and that people would recognize those virtues and work with the same standards. What an idiot I had been!

I continued to have that feeling of gloom and detachment from my partners. While on a business trip to coordinate the opening of new offices in Dublin, Ireland, I visited a beautiful square on St. Stephens Green. As I sat watching the water and the world go by, I decided to give myself a real "dose of my own medicine." As a qualified coach, I believe that more than 90 percent of the answers we seek lie within. I always asked my athletes what they believed the answers to their problems were. I used this principle in my business ventures in the early '80s. As we developed our sales and media group, I asked my young, up-and-coming stars, "What do you think?" I was sitting on that Irish park bench in the afternoon sun. I took out my journal and wrote one line at the top of a blank page:

"How much is enough for me?"
I looked at the open space on the page and my ideas started to flow, slowly at first, answering my own questions. "How much time, how much effort, how much commitment was enough for me?" Then I found myself shifting perspective and asking myself, "What do I not want to do any more? What do I want to do? What would I never do again? Which people would I refuse to work with again? What was I no longer prepared to stand for?"

Instead of gloom and darkness, I focused on what I wanted and what I no longer would accept in my life. I wrote for more than an hour until I had my own freely chosen foundation plan for the future. As I sat there, it was as though someone had released the straps of a large backpack from my shoulders and the burden and weight of the previous months dropped away.

At that moment, the name of a new business came to me. I loved working with people who aimed at better things, so I decided I would work with those who desired success. If they were searching for something better, faster or more reliable, I would coach and help them. I had been doing just that since 1976, in schools, in colleges and on sales teams.

On a wooden bench in a Dublin park, The Aspiration Company was born. Since that day, I have lived the life of which most people only dream. I wrote my dream down on paper and committed to living it out the rest of my life.

Tony Whittle

RETURNING HOME
Jeanne Hugoe-Matthews

The Merry-Go-Round

Have you ever spent a day like this? I have. You drive to work in peak-hour traffic, but you don't remember how you got there. You realize you operated on autopilot because you were worrying whether your cash flow would cover payroll.

You arrive late for a meeting with a supplier who wants immediate settlement of accounts, battle with an overflowing inbox, skip lunch and have next to no time to chat with a supervisor whose partner is seriously ill.

You're lucky to leave the office before 9:00 p.m. and head for the supermarket. On the way there, you realise you left your shopping list on the kitchen counter. You spend a frantic 15 minutes buying an unrelated assortment of groceries and hope to throw a meal together. When you get home, you give up and order out, gulp the food without really tasting it, then collapse in front of the TV with a large glass of red wine.

Your "down time" involves goal setting; planning, reviewing actions and correcting your course; networking; unleashing and dealing with information overload from newspapers, the Internet, books, radio, TV and podcasts; juggling mobile phones and pagers—going, going, going. Always in motion.

A Bare Existence

This existence—I hesitate to call it living—gives us little time to tune into our mental and physical selves. We connect even less with what is happening around us.

Multi-tasking to extremes scatters our efforts to a dozen directions at once. It blurs our focus, dilutes our results and, sooner or later, increases our stress levels. When we fall into bed exhausted, we're still on the merry-go-round. We stare at the ceiling at 2:00 a.m., and realize our memories and thoughts are stimulating stress responses, too.

Stress suppresses our immune systems, making us more vulnerable to chronic infections and poor wound healing. It plays a role in depression, anxiety, coronary heart disease, irritable bowel syndrome and diabetes. Stress can also aggravate chronic fatigue syndrome (CFS). In fact, it can trigger CFS relapses and is a key factor in symptom variability.

In these circumstances, it is tempting to give up or criticize ourselves for being foolish. Perhaps we justify our behaviour and run even harder to stay ahead of the game. However, these responses don't overcome the real challenge: our ongoing busyness. Eventually, we have to pay the piper.

One way to cope is to filter the data that bombards us. We have the unconscious ability to process vast amounts of information, but our conscious minds struggle with the burden. We distort, generalize and delete information to fit our expectations, values and beliefs. As a result, we shroud our lives in uniform greyness. We lose touch with our world and ourselves. We simply exist, rather than living up to our potential, and a little voice inside each of us cries, "Stop the merry-go-round. I want to go home."

Being in the Moment
The best way of stopping the merry-go-round is to be in the moment. For me, being in the moment means being completely present to what is—the here and the now of my life. In the moment, I'm truly alive and experience life to its fullest: pain and joy, tears and laughter, challenges and achievements. While I'm in the moment, I don't judge my experiences. Instead, I am able to remember I'm one with the infinite potential that sustains our universe. I am grateful.

All possibilities are accessible. My responses are no longer hasty but measured. My actions become more compassionate and useful. Free of my mental clutter, I'm able to connect with others and share a moment with them. In a video store, I swap grins with a little boy perched on his father's shoulders. In a railway station, I remember to congratulate the stationmaster on his spotless waiting room. A small miracle unites three women in a store: We laugh as unexpected rain drenches a street during a drought.

When I am present to myself and to the world, I transform my experiences. I allow myself to see, hear, taste, touch and smell the world as it really is. Even eating a meal at home can become a peak experience. I inhale the aroma of a favorite dish, admire the food arranged on my plate, feel and taste it in my mouth and enjoy a conversation with my family or a friend. Through these experiences, I reconnect with my body. I return home.

While in the moment, I have space and freedom to contact my inner wisdom, the aspect of me that is one with the heart and mind of God. I'm able to plan and complete tasks that might otherwise overwhelm me. I can also recognize when I should take time to rest and care for myself. In the now, stress dissolves and is replaced by relaxation, renewal and grace.

Events move more smoothly when I am in the now. I pay closer attention and notice opportunities for cooperation with others. We pool resources and efforts and achieve joint outcomes. I find items I have misplaced in my busyness. Even traffic lights seem to turn green on demand.

Entering into the Moment
How do we enter into the moment?

I believe mindfulness is the answer. We can practice mindfulness, or awareness, when we run, meditate or play with our children. A friend of mine has learned life lessons from observing his cat.

I've found a number of doorways into the moment, some quite ordinary. For example, walking on the beach is similar to the Zen practice of sweeping the floor. There is only the feeling of sand subsiding under my feet, the special quality of light at sunrise, the tang of salt in the air and on my tongue, and the sound of fishermen chatting on the pier.

The merry-go-round stops. I step off, relax and achieve clarity. My daily commitments will soon test my serenity, but for now, all is well. I'm home.

shalom

gentle sun
soft wind
waves shush and hiss
froth white lace against warm sand

blessed space

to dream
to wonder
to be

still

Jeanne Hugoe-Matthews

OH, OLIVER! (FROM THE WAKE UP LIVE MOVIE)
Liz Vassey

I was a very, very, very shy kid, when I was three or four. I just didn't talk to strangers and I was very uncomfortable in front of groups.

I started acting when I was nine, and I started in theater—actually musical theater. It was then that I saw my sister in a play, and I went to my mom, and I said, "I think I would really like to try that." She said, "Oh, I think that would be great. I'm not taking you. Your sister can take you out. I don't want any part of seeing you get up on that stage and seeing what happens."

The first play I auditioned for was *Oliver* and I sang for it, and I played Oliver. I remember getting up on that stage and actually feeling very much at home for the first time.

Once you've had that moment, I would say you have to be incredibly persistent. Do not believe too much of the good or of the bad. Stay true to yourself because they are trying to change you and fix you and mold you. I think what's different or peculiar about you is what's special about you in the first place. Don't lose it.

Liz Vassey

THE DAY I WAS SET FREE
Sharla Evans

As you begin the journey into the depths of who you are, you may be in darkness. Your light might be on its last flicker or you may be in the shadows of your flame. Wherever you may be, soon you will light your candle, see your vision, hear your calling, feel your burning desire and illuminate the world with your light!

A young, slender, brown lady, fresh into adulthood stands inside a government building. The sign to her right reads "Children's Aid Society." She has spent the past 11 years of her life in a system that clothed her, fed her and provided shelter for her. Her time is up, for she had reached the age at which her contract had been terminated. She is handed her very last paycheck for being in foster care.

She is set free and is now on her own. Deep down, she knows she has much to offer this world she is about to coldly enter. But with no parents, family or mentors to turn to, and with no life plan, she wonders what will become of her. Nobody has prepared her for this moment. What direction will she take?

Hi, my name is Sharla Evans, and this is a true story about me.

What is my life purpose? This is a question I often asked myself. I spent a lot of time being very curious about life, this planet, how the world works, who I was and what my role and true purpose were. Since I didn't have parents or family around to answer all of my burning questions, I looked to the world. I remember asking questions in school that my teachers couldn't always answer, but I knew the answers would come some day. I also wanted to know the way to my true self. I wanted to feel complete. I often felt alone in this quest, as if everyone had access to this secret wisdom—these secret answers—and that this wisdom was passed down from parents, which I was short of.

As I matured, I never lost that childlike curiosity. My quest to find the answers to these burning life questions had led me to read many books and to travel and explore many wonderful towns, cities, provinces and countries. I am very much a people person and have many close friends from all over the world: Africa, Poland, Greece, Italy, India, Vietnam, China, Japan, Iran, Canada and United States. I always embrace diversity.

To my surprise, one of my most amazing discoveries was that we all ask ourselves these very questions, regardless of gender, age, social status, type of life lived or experiences had. It seems to be an individual and universal quest! However, it wasn't until I journeyed to the most beautiful place I had ever been that I found what I was looking for.

The Journey to My Inner Guide
I didn't need to take a trip to an exotic place or country to find this ancient, secret wisdom. Instead, I got a first-class ticket to my living room.

That day is still very clear in my mind. I sat cross-legged on the floor with my eyes closed and silently whispered, "Today, in this very moment, I light my internal candle. I acknowledge myself as a unique individual on this earth. In this very moment, I open my body, heart, mind and soul to communicate with me about my life purpose, passions and pleasures. I opened myself to receiving the innate wisdom that I have had since birth. I acknowledge the presence of this wisdom in this very moment. When I connect with myself, I connect with the magnificent universe filled with the infinite possibilities within me."

With each breath that I took, the words, "Just be with you," came into my mind. I remained in this state for what felt like hours. So much love and wisdom flooded my entire being. Then my eyes opened unannounced. I felt complete and whole.

In that moment, I felt like I had just graduated to a new level.

The more that I stayed connected with what I now call my *Inner Guide*—which is the mind, body, heart and soul connection—the more I could hear something deep within me whispering, "See your vision, hear your calling, feel your burning desire, dream big and be the author of your life!"

I devoted a lot of time to getting to know my authentic self and all I had to do was travel within myself and connect with my *Inner Guide*. It was then that I began to feel at home in the world, just like that old saying, "Home is where the heart is." Where your heart is, so are your dreams!

My inner guide showed me the way to my dreams. Through my inner journey, I also discovered that my life challenges were just a gateway to something profound and connected to my life purpose.

I am now a Certified Human Development Coach, Inner Journey Guide, author, and creator of the Light Your Candle Inner Journey Book Program™. I assist others in finding their way to their inner guide and true essence.

There is No Separation Between Your Life Purpose and the Present Moment
When you are connected to your inner guide—mind, body, heart and spirit—you are in the present moment. A deep connection is made and you feel more alive than ever before! This is what it's all about. Living on purpose truly means being present to all of yourself! In this state of being, you have access to the unlimited resources within you. I refer to this as your true essence. I believe there really is no one life purpose, but a series of them. In everything I do, whether it's being a friend or a coach, writing or cooking, I give inspiration and remind others of their greatness. This is my true unique essence and my purpose that runs through everything I do.

So I Ask You...

What has been patiently waiting deep within you to hear, to see, to feel, to taste and to be? Would you like to journey to the depths and discover your true self? Would you like to remember how great you truly are? Would you like to connect to your passion, purpose or authentic self? Would you like to make a difference in the world? If you had a gift you could give to the world, what might it be? The first step is to journey within, connect with your inner guide, light your candle and see your true vision for your life, hear your calling, feel your burning desire!

Perhaps you are beginning to listen to the voice within you that is saying, "I deserve a better life. I deserve to live out my dreams!" If we all lit our authentic candles, how much brighter this world would truly be!

Sharla Evans

KEEPING MY MIND IN THE NOW
Tony Galliano, M.B.A.

At age 16, I found myself living in a dilapidated Datsun station wagon, having been abandoned by my mother who had lost her job and moved 200 miles away to find better opportunities.

My estranged father was continually hospitalized or incarcerated throughout my teenage years. His minor crimes, such as driving under the influence and disorderly conduct, eventually led to more serious offenses such as aggravated assault.

As his health and mental capacity deteriorated, my father became increasingly violent. He eventually went to prison for holding a woman hostage at gunpoint during a drunken rage. After he was paroled, he claimed to be rehabilitated, but continued to suffer from numerous psychological and physical disorders including multiple chemical dependencies, cirrhosis, chronic depression, ulcers, blackouts and dementia.

Where had my life gone wrong? It wasn't always this way; it started out much better. I was identified as "gifted" in the second grade and was enrolled in a special accelerated program in my school district. I was later placed in a magnet school where I excelled in math and science. After completing all available math coursework, my junior high school provided me with a university math professor to build my skills, leading me to the California State "Math Counts" competition.

In high school, I was very active in several organizations: Key Club (vice president, then lieutenant governor of the California-Nevada-Hawaii District), and Junior Statesmen of America and Astronomy Club. In addition to competing in three sports, my academic ability made me a National Hispanic Merit Scholar. Now, as I saw my world crumble around me, I decided to take charge, refused to play the victim, and started *living in the now!* I was determined to survive by working at an oil refinery by day and washing dishes by night. Through a combination of night school and community college, I received my high school diploma by the time I was 18.

I then received three scholarships which funded my first two years of school at Kemper Military Junior College. I embraced living in the now by getting involved in every activity possible, including marching band, concert band, small-bore rifle team, drill team, campus MP and Pershing Rifles Military Fraternity. In addition to holding leadership positions as a platoon leader, ROTC training officer and band officer, I was selected to join the prestigious Scabbard and Blade Military Honor Society.

After junior college, my father's health deteriorated and lead to his death. I was left to handle a mountain of debt as well and the responsibility of supporting his new family who had depended on his disability income. After only a year, I was able to close out the estate and help his family get on their feet.

Eager to make up for lost time, I completed my undergraduate degree in 17 months at Wichita State University, graduating *cum laude* while working 20 plus hours per week. During this short time, I was elected University Ombudsman (third in the student government chain of command), competed on the varsity rowing team and served on multiple university committees. I then served my country as an infantry officer in the U.S. Army.

After sustaining multiple injuries, I received an honorable medical discharge from the Army. I found immediate success as I transitioned into the corporate world. In my first seven years, I received six meritorious promotions in areas of leadership development, sales and marketing. I also became the second youngest graduate in the history of Emory University's #6 ranked Modular Executive M.B.A. program.

As I launched several multi-billion dollar healthcare products, I made an amazing discovery. Most people do not have the ability to change behavior, even when their lives depends on it. In fact, 90 percent of patients receiving heart bypass surgery do not change their lifestyles after the surgery, even though they know that their lives depend on it. Similar statistics are true for people battling cancer, diabetes, cholesterol, hypertension, obesity and HIV.

Thus began my quest to understand why it is so easy for me to achieve my goals while everyone else struggles to do so. During collaboration with Dr. Goutam Challagalla (Georgia Institute of Technology) on a project, he recognized my passion for research and introduced me to many research leaders from top institutions around the world. My hard work and research finally paid off when I was asked to create a marketing leadership development curriculum for Abbott Laboratories. My team was able to work with superstars like Seth Godin, Keith Ferrazzi and Philip Kotler, just to name a few.

Only by combining my background and resources with a comprehensive global network have I been able to fully develop the science behind 60secondstrategist.com. I work daily with a strong cadre of advisers from the business and academic communities to help people overcome mental obstacles and achieve their dreams.

Driven by my passion for 60 Second Strategist research and the desire to impact the world, I work to help others overcome any deficiency or obstacle they may experience in life.

My research has taught me that our thinking usually fails for three reasons:
- Our thinking is driven by our "cognitive unconscious," where we have already formed mental maps that become our points of reference from which we look at the world. Most of the time, we are unaware of these mental maps and the impact they have.
- Our thinking is physically and firmly ingrained in us. This is reinforced by the structure and very nature of the brain itself.

- Isolated facts have little effect on changing behavior. If the fact does not fit the current mind-set, it is instantly rejected.

What can you do to shift your thinking?

Define and analyze your thinking by asking yourself:
- What influences are shaping my thought patterns?
- What recent decisions have been influenced by this way of thinking?
- How has my own education and experience shaped my thoughts?

Challenge your thinking by asking yourself:
- Why do I hold unproductive thought patterns and why won't I let go of them?
- What are some of the barriers that might be keeping me from changing?
- What are the challenges and opportunities in exploring a new way of thinking?

Discuss your thinking by asking yourself:
- How do others see it?
- How do my feelings and emotions drive my behavior?
- Who can I talk with to gain greater clarity of the situation at hand?

Develop a plan by asking yourself:
- Should I change my current thinking? How?
- In what way is my current thinking working or not working for me?
- How can I change or modify my current thinking to improve results?

With the launch of 60secondstrategist.com, I am able to offer free resources that I have spent millions of dollars and a lifetime to acquire. I continue to draw from my unique experiences to effectively collaborate with leaders and organizations worldwide to help make the world a better place, one mind at a time!

Tony Galliano, M.B.A.

LIVING IN THE NOW
R. Winn Henderson, M.D.

Try as you may, there is no way to change the past. Yesterday's circumstances become one of two things: excess baggage you drag with you every step you take for the rest of your life, or building blocks for the future. You paint a dull picture for your future if you become so attached that you cannot let go of past events that have negatively affected your life. Obviously, the best option is to glean from them the lessons they taught you and use these lessons to choose a better way to live. The central value of the past is that you learn from it, but equally important is that we learn to live in the here and now without looking over our shoulder with constant "what-if" scenarios running through our heads.

Please don't go through life filled with regrets for things that happened to you. They happened for a reason. The old saying, "If it doesn't kill you, it will make you stronger," (Friedrich Nietzsche) takes on new meaning if you break down your past with all the positives and negatives that have influenced how you view your future. Even the worst scenario can be positive if you learn from it.

We make choices every day of our lives. We can easily remember the most important things that have happened in our lives thus far. So why not look at even the bad things as blessings, because they happened to teach a lesson? You would not be where you are today without these things in your life. You are in the "now" of your life.

Forgiveness is terribly important when considering the past. Learning to forgive may be the most important lesson we are meant to learn. We do not know why things happen unless we are able to determine the importance of these things in our lives. However, we do know that we were born with all of the tools we need to get through life. Our creator loved us enough to equip us with these tools so we could learn from life experiences. He wants each and every person on the planet to live a full and wonderful life.

Why do bad things happen to good people? This is a question negative people constantly use as a crutch to validate their own personal views of the world. They say, "Why should I try when all around me I see bad things happening to good people?"

What we need to remember is that our creator gave us all the gifts we need to learn from life. This includes the free will to do as we choose. Spiritually enlightened individuals make use of their free will to view even the negative things in life as beneficial. They do not necessarily allow the negative things to drag them down. They learn and become even stronger. They live life in the present—the now. Watch these people process the bad things that happen to them.

Possibly the most important factor when reviewing our past is to remember nothing that has happened to us is so terrible that we are beyond redemption. Whether we caused the event from our personal use of free will, or whether it was something negative someone else introduced into our lives, there is always an option we can take.

Great men and women through the ages have set examples for us to follow. An example that comes to mind is Jesus Christ. Something negative was coming into His life from the outside (crucifixion). Jesus had the option of doing any number of things that would have saved him the pain and suffering. However, He took this "negative" and turned it into the most positive action I can think of in the course of history. He taught the nature of love and forgiveness with His last breath.

We can look around us today and find wonderful people who espouse the same loving and forgiving nature. These people process the negatives in their lives and find a way to grow stronger as a result. They are determined to have a good outlook on the future. They share a common thread, knowing they are what they think about. They learn lessons from the negatives in their lives and then file them away and leave them in the past. They do not create baggage that weighs them down in the present. They look to the future and rise above the negativity of the past to live lives that are destined to become positive influences in the world.

When you pick a role model for your life, find one that has a track record for optimism. View your mentor's total life story. See the way he or she choses to live his or her life. It may have been the result of some dramatic, life-changing event that opened your mentor's eyes to a better way to live. Regardless of the reason why this person chose to look at life positively and optimistically, by doing so your mentor has the potential to change lives (more specifically, your life). By example, others see the kind of life that leads to contentment, happiness and peace of mind. Choose your mentors well.

Now look at yourself the same way. Ask the questions, "Do I want to be a positive influence on the people in my life? Do I want the very best for those people I love and care about?" Look beyond your close inner circle of friends and relatives. You are a part of a bigger picture.

The ripple effect emanating from a person's thoughts and actions has an effect on the universe as a whole. There are ebbs and flows of positive and negative energy, and our job is to become a part of the positive energy flow in order to change the world in a positive way.

You are sitting at a crossroads in your life when you find yourself looking back. You can either live in the past and carry your baggage, or learn from life and move forward. I hope you choose to join those who truly live enthusiastically, in the present, and have the wonderful, loving, peaceful "now" that your Creator wants for you. You are unique and deserve only the best. The choice is entirely up to you. I would encourage you to use all the tools at your disposal to create that future, not only for yourself, but for others who see you as their mentor.

See yourself as someone who can change the world, because you can! You are a unique, creative process in the making. Your life can become a thing of beauty through love by blending in with others who share positive visions. Together, the rainbow formed from this interaction can brighten many lives. Never doubt for a single moment how valuable you are.

Compared to the universe, humans may seem like minute particles of sand. However, each grain has great meaning to the Creator. He instilled in each of His wonderful creations special gifts and talents to accomplish His plan for mankind. The greatest gift we were given was the gift of love. As we are bathed in love by our Creator, we are equipped with everything we need to make a positive influence and impact on the world.

Since life is precious, make each second count. Respect your "now" and live it fully, because that is essentially all you have. Make each day the very best you can. Learn to make good, positive choices in life by looking at the "big picture." Prayer and meditation can be so very valuable in this respect.

You are in the "now" phase of your life. Tap into all the resources at your disposal to make your dreams come true. Recognize your value as a child of God. Use the past as a lesson that will help you graduate into a new world where you realize there is nothing you cannot do. After all, we are limited only by our own thoughts of limitation.

Realize love is the primary thing that will make the world a better place in which to live. Love can never be underrated. It is the thing that keeps our world turning in a positive direction.

We all came from the same place. We share the same Heavenly Father, and we are all precious in His sight. May you have a bright and wonderful future filled with the peace, love and happiness you so richly deserve.

R. Winn Henderson, M.D.

BY GOD, ANYTHING I CAN DO, YOU CAN DO, TOO!
C. E. Molyneaux

If you have watched election night coverage on CBS with Dan Rather or Katie Couric reporting you have seen my work. I do systems integration and election graphics controls with a world-class team. The touch-screen Dan and Katie use, the pictures of the winners, the pie charts, bar charts and maps are just tips of the visual iceberg my team and I innovated to give America election results. There are only a handful of people in the world who can handle the intensity of the political, technological and creativity demands to get this job done. Stars may come and go in TV and movies, but consistency of excellence is a kind of behind-the-scenes stardom that endures. But this was not always so.

At 16, I was hacking on the school DEC computer years before Steve Jobs made his first trip to India to later create the first Apple computer. I was very good at programming for my age. Other kids played sports while I played with the computer. This was my passion. I was having so much fun! I was even interviewed on the radio when I graduated from high school, but the college financial aid promised by my stepfather never materialized, so my career languished.

At 18, I was married to the most wonderful girl on earth with a fine son, but no career opportunities and no education past high school. I tried to become a car mechanic, an electrician and a self-employed window cleaner. Our house even burned down and we had no insurance. We lost everything but our car, the clothes on our backs, a few tools and some pictures. At one time, I was so broke, my wife and I had to share one can of tomato soup a day. That was all we had for many weeks. I still have scars on both of my inner forearms from donating plasma alongside drunks for money to pay for cans of tomato soup, milk for our son, and gas for the car so I could find more cleaning customers.

Once, I had only $20 in my pocket, and I had to choose between food in my stomach or gas in my car so I could open a new territory for business. I chose the gas, opened a new location that day and came home with more gas for the next day and food to eat that night. Desperate to get into college to earn my computer degree, I finally joined the USAF and served to obtain the GI Bill. Meanwhile, I fixed F-15s in Germany and New Mexico, learning a great deal about hardware and software. I also learned what "mission critical" meant, because a pilot's life depended daily on the quality of work I did on his plane. I also learned what "working hard" meant, as 12-hour shifts to drill for war were commonplace. To this day, I work from the time I wake up until the minute I go to bed, six days a week and even seven when those I serve need me.

I went to college, obtained my bachelor's degree in computer science and built flight simulators for a while. Because of my technical background, I ended up as a pre-sales analyst at an emerging high-tech California company. I must have read more than 100 success books and personally had a chat with noted author Brian Tracy in the mid 1980s. I rounded out my skills by learning how to speak effectively in public, dress for success, and deal with office politics. Among other things, I innovated breakthroughs in satellite data processing for NASA, revolutionized much of the flight simulation industry and was called upon to create a world's first broadcast effect for CBS in 1994, when 10 other companies told the network it was impossible. I did all of this while earning my M.B.A. part-time. In 1996, CBS was awarded an Emmy significantly based upon my personal contributions and advisement. I am still having a blast as I write this a decade later. My wife, the jewel that she is, has stuck with me through thick and thin. I now help my adult son off and on, with various other fun projects on the Web.

Things to consider? Like a child, when you experience your first love of something, go back to it. Find a way to make it your life's career if you can, because that is where your heart really is. If you're working only 40 hours at what you do, it's not the fun thing you should be doing.

Change what you do and have fun 60 hours a week. You'll make more money while playing at what you love, involving your family in the process. Mission critical means helping those you serve to become as successful as they can be, with a focus on them, their needs and their success first, not yours first.

Never lose sight of the vision of what you can be, despite all that life throws at you. Keep plugging. Where there is a will, there is a way, and that is no cliché. Plan your work and work your plan, because that is what keeps it all organized. Then cross every "t" and dot every "i" and relish in the accomplishment of even the smallest of critical details. Many efforts are like programming, which are exercises by imperfect human beings to create the perfect. Only by passionate vision, superb planning and outstanding execution is world-class possible. No doubt, there are more firsts I plan to do!

For those who say you cannot work at business and succeed with a family, I say that is not so. My family relationships improved me because my successes are also shared, based on the foundation of strength that came from my family. God is the source of all that is good, pure and perfect in the universe and in me. I am certainly no one special and started out on a far less than stellar path. We all can be more than we think we can!

Reality is the same for you as it is for me. If you get nothing else out of this, at least get this much. By God, anything I have done in my field, you can do in yours, too! Your field may not be software, but it matters not what it is. Whether your career is at home, in a business or in a corporation, you will be at your best when you synchronize your passions, talents, vision, strategy and implementation with reality. That's all I chose to do and you can choose it, too! Then, serve all those you serve with all of the energy that you can muster. You'll never look back, while having the time of your life along the way!

C. E. Molyneaux

A CALL TO A LIFE PURPOSE
Veronica Sauter, Ph.D.

I t was early in life, I recall. I was perhaps four or five years old. Everything seemed so crystal clear. Colors vibrated. Lights glistened, as if a battery powered their every flicker. Sounds reverberated, music danced in my head. Every voice I heard remained engraved in my ears for life. Life was full. I saw auras around people, plants and puppies. My senses were my toys. Perception was the game.

My teen years were fun and carefree until one day during my senior year in Catholic high school. The classroom door opened and the disciplinarian was looking for me. I sensed her presence when she was still in the hallway. She whispered to our teacher, who called me to the front of the room. As I approached, I asked, "Is he still alive?" Sister gasped, and her eyes welled with tears as she replied, "Yes, but you're needed at the hospital. I'll take you there. Your father has been in an accident." She gave no details during the trip that I thought would never end. When I saw my father, a silent voice echoed in my head, *"Care for him."* He was hanging by a golden thread, but skilled doctors saved his life. Still, the road to recovery would be long.

Dad was one of 17 children. He emigrated from Bavaria to the United States on the eve of the Great Depression. He worked hard for a livelihood in his new homeland. Knowing I could help this meek and gentle man who taught me the supreme importance of kindness inspired me. He deserved only the best of care. Caring required a lot of physical work. Early in his journey back to health, I met a young woman who taught me an ancient hands-on modality known as Jin Shin Jyutsu®. Jin Shin harmonizes body, mind and spirit for healing. I wanted to learn whatever I could to help him. While my rudimentary training at the time proved effective in restoring his vitality, it was my clear intention for his healing and the innocent love of a child for a parent that yielded the best results. Slowly, he recovered.

After college, I decided to work in pharmaceutical sales. The world economy of 1975 derailed that dream, so I immediately entered graduate school to earn a master's degree in Spanish literature. Certainty sustained me when ridicule came from many who considered literature as a rather useless field unless one wanted to teach. Criticism could not dissuade me. Latin and the Spanish language resonated with me. They were my passion. Later, language skills served me well during the many years I traveled Europe and Latin America in medical sales. Once, while traveling in Germany, an elderly gentleman fell at the train station. Alone, his devoted wife could not help him to his feet. As I added my strength to hers, the stranger arose. I assisted this couple as if they were my own parents. Time and space vanished. That night when I called home, my mother told me Dad had fallen. She didn't know how she would be able to help him to his feet, but *somehow* she did it!

Fifteen years after the tragic accident, the day arrived when my dad began to slip away. It would not be long. On that August night, I placed a cool cloth on his warm forehead as he rested. I closed my eyes. Suddenly, the two of us were traveling through a tunnel of blinding, scintillating light. The "speed of light" was almighty. Almighty is light. When Dad and I reached a portal, he passed through. Some invisible gatekeeper tacitly denied me entry. Immediately, I began my retreat back to the physical reality of our home. My feet were still burning and my heart was pounding. My dad's pulse was very slow and his breathing shallow. When Mom came downstairs that morning, I told her of our experience. "Daddy is still breathing, but his soul has gone to Heaven already," I said. "He will die today."

Months passed and 1986 ended. Time healed our pain and life went on. We adjusted. One summer day, after finishing work at a local Philadelphia hospital, I decided to find something for dinner. A metaphysical bookshop stood just a few doors from the quaint Greek restaurant where I was headed. Some unseen force, a hand on my shoulder, firmly pushed me into the store. It led me to a bookshelf on the left. I picked up a book, opened to a page and read one paragraph. "This is it," I thought. I purchased the book, then proceeded to find the Mediterranean fare.

For more than a year, I would pick up that book and reread passages and entire chapters before returning it to my bookshelf. The principles of healing that it represented belonged to another world—a world diametrically opposed to mainstream medicine. I rationalized why I should not change careers. An uncharted course demanded a trusting heart.

Barbara Brennan's *Hands of Light,* the book to which I had been directed so mysteriously, coaxed me to pursue the healing profession. Finally, it won me over. By 1991, I enrolled in a four-year program to develop high-sense perception and healing skills that addressed the subtle energy body. There is no doubt in my mind that it was my father's spirit that guided me to that specific book.

At healing school, one method we learned addressed aligning life's purpose. After years in operating rooms where I observed surgical procedures to repair fractures and severe traumatic head injuries, and to reconstruct congenital cranial deformities, I was performing bioenergetic techniques very similar to those I had routinely witnessed. The surgical instruments I used consisted of my own energetic hands—rearranging subtle bodies made of photons—packets of light moving in waveforms. These etheric constructs are the blueprints for the real, physical body. My thesis was on how the geometric principles used in "earthly" three-dimensional surgery are based on sacred geometry, the perennial shapes which form all matter. This is how I have come to facilitate the "enlightened purpose" for others. Sometimes, the dark contrast of disease and pain ignite enlightenment.

Long ago, the word *vocation* implied a spiritual calling. It derives from the Latin *vocatio,* or "summons." *Vocare* means "to call" and comes from *vox,* or "voice." Spirit's call is subtle, yet it is persistent. Listen for its whisper. Hush the mind, focus on others, resolve to contribute to the highest good for humankind. Spirit paves the path. It's not hard work. True purpose is effortless. Our life purpose is with us always. Think of it as a spiritual GPS of divine design!

Consciousness focuses our vision. Awakening to our "call" refocuses us each day. If we expand attention and enlarge our perspective to include others—embracing a broader cause—the heart opens and compassion steps in. Limiting self-doubt cannot survive in a heart governed by loving compassion. Conviction of doing what is right helps us stay our course. Faith that we are infinite beings capable of miracles fosters in us a greatness needed to co-create a new world of hope and peace.

Veronica Sauter, Ph.D.

LIGHT, TRUTH AND FREEDOM
George Hinestrosa

"Give me liberty or give me death." These courageous words, spoken by Patrick Henry during his famous speech in 1775, denouncing slavery, have become the standard by which we, as a free nation, live— or do we? While physical bondage and outward abuse have been brought under control by a better understanding of human dignity and respect for life, as individuals we have succumbed to the enslavement and bondage of the mind and will. "How so?" you might ask. In order to better understand this point, consider what Jesus said to the crowd as they accused Him: "You shall know the truth, and the truth shall set you free" (John 8:32). Interestingly, the crowd retaliated, saying that they were sons and daughters of Abraham and had never been in bondage. What was the message intended for them? What freedom, if not from physical bondage, was Jesus referring to?

Through adolescence, we have various experiences caused through contact with other people and situations. Beginning with our parents and relatives, the first years of our lives are flooded with experiences that are shaped through and by their own early adolescent lessons.

Next, we learn from our friends and teachers. As we enter adulthood, our co-workers become an influence as well. Through these influences, we learn a variety of emotions such as kindness, playfulness, love, hate, envy, jealousy and friendship. These are internalized and adopted to our own character predisposition, which according to psychological research, fits into a combination of about 12 different types.

Mass media and the Internet have, over the last 15 years, become our preferred means of communication. These forms of communication, while being wonderful scientific breakthroughs, have also opened avenues of information and marketing that allow nearly spontaneous influence upon our minds and will, but how does this occur? These energies are electrical currents and waves of sound that come through the media and for the most part seem harmless. However, with continuous repetition and our inattention to the ease by which habits can be formed, our thinking patterns and ways of life are molded. One also hears and reads of habits being referred to as paradigms or paradigm shifts. These shifts in reality become spontaneous and we end up acting and thinking in a given way that may or may not necessarily represent our true potential. The end result is a shaping of our way of looking at situations, people, the world and life in general. The final state of mind-conditioning may not actually be in our best interest as we attempt to live the life we want or wish to live.

At this point in our lives, we begin to contemplate who we are, what our purpose in life is, and how we can make a difference. This is the point where few people actually realize there is a better, higher way of life worth striving for. Still others, because of ingrained habits, drift back into their customary ways of living, thinking and searching, in order to add meaning to their lives through material gain and competition. The "rat race" becomes the norm.

Understanding our minds and the way our brains process information through the senses, and then striving to understand the unseen spiritual and natural laws that govern our universe are of paramount importance. "Group-think" can be good or bad, depending upon the origin of its transmission and the end state desired. Centers of private and public education, religion and the free market all have an end state that they are programmed to influence and produce. In the Bible, Solomon said, "Guard your heart with all diligence, for out of it are the issues of life" (Proverbs 4:23).

What, then, is the truth that may set us free? When Jesus spoke again to the people, he said, "I am the light of the world. Whoever follows me will never walk in darkness, but will have the light of life" (John 8:12). Truth is light. What light, though? Jesus spent his life teaching in parables. If we read and study His teachings as they pertain to the natural laws, as well as the laws of thought and spirit, we find that He was teaching humanity to take control of the way they view things. He taught, "Ask and you shall receive, seek and you will find, knock and it shall be opened unto you, sow and you shall reap what you sow," (Matt. 21:22, Luke 11:9, Gal. 6:7) and clearly stated, "As a man thinks, so he is" (Galatians 6:7).

In light of this, we find that some of us unconsciously adopt these patterns of thought, while others sporadically use them, and still others totally ignore the fact that these laws exist at all. We need to continuously use the correct patterns to create our daily lives so that we will have perfect order. We may say, then, that the truth lies in understanding the natural and spiritual laws and the light is likened to the knowledge of facts that affects us. Our level of freedom or bondage (mental spirituality) is in direct relation to that understanding. The questions then become, "What level or category of enlightenment have we adopted? What are we striving for? Have we enslaved ourselves willingly by allowing our minds to be influenced?"

To renew your life daily, begin to sow only the best seeds in your mind and watch them grow into the fruitful life you desire!

George Hinestrosa

NEVER QUIT! NEVER TOO LATE!
Dr. Ruth Diamond

Do you know anyone whose "real" life began at 70 and whose life is still expanding at 80? If not, you soon will! My big dream started at age four. A doctor hurt me so badly that I decided I wanted to become a doctor who would never hurt anyone. I have now been a doctor for more than 55 years and my dream is still expanding. I am passionately living the life I love. I want to share with you that life is long and you're never too old to learn. It's very important to realize that anger can be a catalyst for good only if it helps us locate and overcome problems. Anger should be directed at the problem and never at oneself or others.

When I reached 70, patients were saying to me, "You should be retired," which angered me. I have a mission statement: "I'm going out of this life still growing and learning." I kept learning, and by 75, my patients were saying, "We need you! Don't retire!"

My family emigrated from Holland to Australia in 1939, when I was 10. We had nowhere to live until a war veteran of 62 took us in and provided for us. Sadly, this family friend secretly abused me, resulting in nightmares for two years. After this incident, we moved to Sydney, where my father joined the Air Force. When I was 13, he had a terrible accident that permanently paralyzed him and affected his speech. He was tremendously frustrated and became mentally ill. Our family suffered as he was certified, paroled and discharged, causing the whole saga to be repeated.

During my teenage years, my favorite expression was, "Joie de Vivre." I longed for the "Joy of Living." I was my mother's "right hand," dependable, studious and energetic. Yet, something was always missing—I was too inwardly focused. It has taken me a long time to see that life doesn't revolve around me, which is such an important lesson.

At age 13, I sewed, studied and worked jobs. Yet, I was lonely and always seeking approval and acceptance. I was a human "doing" rather than a human "being." I still wanted to be a doctor and loved to read medical biographies. By age 15, I visited a doctor who constantly told me, "Medicine is no career for a woman!" This was terribly discouraging! This was during WWII, and I wanted to be on the front line comforting and healing the troops while preparing for science or psychology. I didn't believe in myself and I felt others knew better.

My mother was of a tolerant nature, but my father was strict and religious. I greatly feared him and gradually grew to hate him. I was always respectful, but by the time I started college, I became an atheist. I was deeply angry inside, but I masked that even from myself. It has taken me decades to learn to be emotionally sincere.

I enrolled in the university in 1946, and planned to study science, but when I reached the counter, I blurted out "medicine" and went home jubilant. There were very few women among the 650 medical students. For class, I was paired with a very needy Jewish escapee from Vienna named Peter. By Med 2, he and I had entered a foolish five-year engagement. I was needy and eager to please. In Med 3, I broke off the engagement on two separate occasions because Peter threatened to commit suicide.

Unfortunately, I failed Med 3. To repeat the class meant I had to earn money by working in a factory by day and waitressing by night. I really wanted to be a doctor and I held on to that throughout all the drama. I managed to get a class credit in medical finals despite my father's passing away in the middle of five weeks of exams in 1952. I was finally on my way to being a doctor.

In 1950, I fell in love and was engaged. I became pregnant but was compelled by my fiancé to have an abortion. I felt like a lamb being led to the slaughter. We were both medical students and pregnancy was forbidden. We married in 1953, but it wasn't a good relationship. We had a son in 1954, and I became pregnant again in 1958. I also became inwardly suicidal. Why? Because four days before our second son was born, I discovered my husband's infidelity. I felt I had to leave him despite the low status of women, no social security and little suitable work. I was an admired doctor but was utterly lost inside. I was in survival mode for five years trying to support two babies and work, all while dealing with the pain and unanswered questions. My confidence was shattered.

I don't know what would have happened if I hadn't found Jesus Christ. At about 1:30 p.m., on February 22, 1959, at the age of 30, I was radically saved by God, converted and changed. I learned to laugh. Medicine no longer controlled me. God gave me the strength to live through those tough, lonely years as a single, working mother.

In 1972, I married my very best friend. He was a Christian and I felt truly loved. I had a country medical practice and newfound confidence. From 1978 to 1990, we built a mission vessel and made it our home. We provided medical and mission services in the South Pacific. I endured awful seasickness, but I loved seeing the wider world. It was all wonderful until I discovered that for the past eight years, my husband had been unfaithful with a female crew member who called us Mum and Dad. It was devastating because she was 40 years younger than I!

After this, I returned to land and resumed work in traditional medicine, heartbroken by life and still desperately seeking that "Joie de Vivre." Finally, at age 70, I came out of a 40-year "identity wilderness." All my knowledge of God and forgiveness became real and I could see God as the loving father I never had. This opened the doorway to alternate medical work. I learned to focus on health, not disease.

So, what next? At 76, I was diagnosed with cancer in the right breast. I felt divinely led to forego an operation. There is still a tumor in my breast four years later, but it has not spread. My new focus is life, purpose, health, nutrition, exercise, sun, forgiveness and supplements. I have continued to work, sharing all I have learned along my journey. Cancer has been a springboard to better medicine. The God I dismissed in my youth has become my strength, help and inspiration.

To be an excellent doctor, one must focus on health, continual learning, forgiveness and leading by example. Very few dare to tell me they are over the hill or past their prime. At 80, I am full of life, learning more every day and loving it. Never give up on yourself. Find your dream, and with God's help, live it!

Dr. Ruth Diamond

NOT BULLET-PROOF
John Assaraf

I have been blessed: at an early age I learned the value of my health. Plenty of people spend two or three decades believing they are "ten feet tall and bullet-proof," but at the age of 17, I was introduced to reality in a major car accident.

For several months, I had no choices concerning my physical condition. Then I started an intensive rehab program. Up until that point, my dream, like that of many other kids, was to play professional basketball. The dream still lingered when, at 21, I was diagnosed with uclerative colitis. I was absorbing 25 pills a day, including cortisone enemas to help with the severe pain and discomfort of that disease.

It doesn't sound like the story of someone who is "blessed," does it? Yet, it is true, and the reason is simple. Long before it was too late and long before I could develop poor habits, I was shown beyond any doubt that God only gave me one body to hang around in. My job is to keep it in the best operating condition that I can. That includes both the physical and mental elements of the self.

I made that discovery when I was young enough to understand that my body is breakable. I decided that I would not be unable to enjoy the quality of my life due to the abuse of this miracle called a body. As I got older I also became aware of the spiritual side of my being. I learned how meditation and calmness allow me to be at peace.

So, today, my regimen includes a daily meditation to connect with the source that created me, along with a workout to keep this body in high gear. I play life to the fullest, and I want this vehicle to last as long as it can. My responsibility is to learn as much as I can about the latest and best practices to make this happen. Prioritizing my physical and mental well-being above work and social concerns allows me to take care of me first.

Is that selfish? I think not, for my belief is that everything we do is better if we do our best.

John Assaraf

RUNNING INTO ENLIGHTENMENT
Chris D. Clausen

While lying on a bench, being treated by Red Cross medical personal, I was surrounded by a crowd of concerned people. I had just completed 87.5 miles of a 100-mile ultra-marathon and was not feeling well. It was 6 a.m. and I had been on my feet for 24 consecutive hours. Both of my feet were painfully swollen and blistered. The blisters had been wrapped with duct tape to keep the skin in place. My legs felt like lead. My head hurt. I didn't think I could go on.

It was easy for anyone in the room to see that my body was hurting. What was not so easy to see was how much my pride was hurting. You see, this was my second attempt at completing a 100-mile ultra-marathon. My first attempt the previous year ended at the 75-mile mark, with medical personnel forcing me to withdraw because I was dehydrated. In that moment of disappointment and failure, I swore I would return and finish this race.

Here I was, a year later, staring failure in the face once again. I had trained hard for a full year. I had a crew of ten friends and family members who had flown from Long Island, New York, to Raleigh, North Carolina to support my quest to finish the Umstead 100 Mile Ultra-Marathon. They had taken turns running with me all day and through the night. Yes, my body hurt, but my pride hurt worse. I was going to let them all down again, or so I thought.

I had not yet met a race volunteer named Sally Squire, a mature, gray-haired woman who, by her own admission, could be the mother of this nearly 50-year-old ultra-runner. She was, however, probably the only person in the room who wasn't feeling sorry for me. As I sat on the bench having my feet tended to, Sally bent down to look me in the eye and said, "Listen, it's going to be a long wait 'til next year's race if you don't finish, so I want you to suck it up, get off this bench and get out the door!"

I was stunned! It was tough love for sure, but she was right. Continuing on with this race was going to hurt like hell, but stopping now was going to be even more painful. I had to finish.

Nearly every decision we make in life is based on whether we believe the outcome will bring us pain or pleasure. There is no doubt we will do much more to avoid pain than we'll ever do to gain pleasure. Sally's "wake-up call" reminded me to consider how painful it would be for me to withdraw and not finish this race.

How often do you allow yourself to feel the pain and disappointment of failure? When you need to be proactive and take action toward a desired outcome, how willing are you to consider the price of inaction? Yes, there are times when just getting started can be uncomfortable or even painful, but chances are, the pain of not starting and not taking action could ultimately be even greater!

It hurt just to stand on my feet. I took one step, then another. The rain that had been falling through the night finally stopped. Before I knew it, I had covered a mile. Then two. Even though my feet still hurt, my body began to feel better. My spirits rose along with the sun (the second sunrise I had seen during this race).

I finished the Umstead 100-Mile Ultra-marathon in 28 hours and 39 minutes to a chorus of cheers from my family and friends. It was one of the most difficult, yet rewarding, experiences I'd ever been through. So many miles, so many life lessons.

The first lesson is that we are all capable of achieving so much more than society, friends and perhaps even family members have pro-grammed us to believe. Many people live their lives limited by false beliefs. If we could only re-program what we believe is possible, we could literally change our lives. Although running 100 miles has a way of changing what you believe is possible, you don't have to go to such extremes.

"If we all did the things we are capable of doing, we would literally astound ourselves."—Thomas Edison, Inventor

In life, as in a long-distance event like the ultra-marathon, you go through periods when you feel like a million bucks and you go through times when you feel like you just want to quit. Sometimes you have to just "suck it up," as Sally told me, get started, get out the door and continue to put one foot in front of another, in spite of how you may be feeling at the moment. If you can do this while keeping an eye on your goal, you significantly increase your chances of achieving whatever it is you are after.

It is not enough to just enjoy crossing the finish line. You have to enjoy the journey. If you can learn to embrace the struggle, you can look forward to challenges as they come your way. This will position you to take advantage of opportunities that may be hidden within.

Fear: Isn't that what limits most people in life? Fear of failure. Fear of rejection. Fear of flying. Fear of having our hearts broken. I'll agree, there are some fears that are good and have helped preserve our species, such as fear of fire and fear of falling. What if we could re-wire ourselves to face our fears? What if we could finally realize that 99 percent of the time we are worrying about things that will never happen?

"A coward dies a thousand deaths. A hero dies but once!"

We can achieve much more in life together than we could ever achieve alone if we align ourselves with others who are of a like mind. I had the advantage of training each weekend with family and friends. I had a wife who fully supported my mission to complete the full 100 miles. Imagine how much more difficult my task would have been if I had a spouse who questioned my actions and friends who not only wouldn't run with me, but ridiculed me for even trying.

Are you surrounded by people who will support you and help get you

WAKE UP... LIVE THE LIFE YOU LOVE

where you want to go in life? If the answer is no, then you have a decision to make. You can either *change* the people you hang with, or you can change the *people* you hang with! Which do you think is easier?

"Keep away from those who try to belittle your ambitions. Small people always do that, but the really great make you feel that you, too, can become great."—Mark Twain

Know what your purpose is. Stay connected to it. Spend more time reminding yourself why your desired outcome is a must and spend less time wondering how you will achieve it. Trust your subconscious mind to take you in the direction you need to go.

At the end of our days, our lives will be either a warning to others or an example of what is possible. We get to decide which it will be by the decisions we make as we live in the now.

Chris D. Clausen

PAGE 72   www.WAKEUPGIFT.COM

BREAKDOWN ON LIFE'S SUPERHIGHWAY
Paul Usher

"When are you coming home, Dad?" my son asked. "I don't know, but we'll get together then," I said. These words are from Harry Chapin's famous song, "Cat's in the Cradle." I can still hear the chords echo in my mind, and I feel nostalgic, like remembering the smell of fairy floss at the fairground.

For over 15 years, my workday began between 4 and 5 a.m. "But it's still dark then, you must be crazy!" people would say. I would smile and inwardly feel guilty knowing that the next half of the day would be just as crazy. I would close the lid of my laptop around 10 p.m., sometimes later. I once saw the ability to survive on little sleep as a blessing, but lately it had become more of a curse.

Some business analysts would call me a one-man army: sales, support, installation, design and development—the lonely life of a wanna-be millionaire in the guise of a software company. "If I can just get this one deal, I know I can work less," was my regular retort to my wife Samantha who often raised an eyebrow when I tried to explain why I had to retreat back to the office.

The years have passed me by, and my body has gone from its one-time beanpole shape into a pear, then finally into jelly. My children, Jarrett, Jaynee, Jaimee, Jordana and Jakob have all grown up knowing me as a "dad-in-a-box," the box being the office that surrounds me hour after hour. That was my life before my wake-up call.

Remember those big, old wind-up alarm clocks with two bells sitting atop a huge, grinning clock face and that little hammer just waiting to launch a cacophony on your unexpecting ears? That was my wake-up call. The week had been trying: clients were demanding; staff demanded more; the children fought for attention over the precious amount of time they had with me and I was getting the all-knowing look from my beautiful wife. I felt as if life itself was getting too hard, but what were my options? I certainly am not a quitter. In short, I was catching every ball that was being thrown at me, regardless of the consequences of dropping one or two to catch the next one.

I recall standing in front of the mirror at 4 a.m., giving myself my morning pep talk. My eyes looked sunken, my body out of shape and my hairline happily showing me where it used to be. Enough was enough. I had listened to plenty of CDs by my digital mentors (Brian Tracy, Jay Abraham and Mark Victor Hansen) in the preceding weeks. Something had to give. Was there merit to anything these guys were saying? One thing I knew for sure: Trying was worth a shot because the alternative certainly was not working.

As the cliché goes, "Today is the first day of the rest of your life" (Charles Dederich), and that day was the day I started shedding those few extra pounds. I decided to join a gym again, but this time would be different. This time, there would be no "get thin quick scheme." I was determined to work toward my goals. This time I wouldn't look for that one killer deal or the "get rich quick scheme." I won't bore you with all the step-by-step processes that followed. I will only say that this time was different and today really was going to be something special. I began doing little things like paying attention when one of the children needed help with a taxing homework question. I set up a personal train-er at the gym and I began to put my life into perspective. I had learned not only to stop and smell the roses, but to watch them grow and change day by day. I learned to appreciate what I had already achieved in life.

One trap I had fallen into was providing substitutes for the children. Whether it was television, Xbox®, Playstation® or the Wii™, the kids had them all. My eldest boy once wrote me an e-mail (yes, that's right, it was easier for him to get to me that way!), and he pointed out, in no uncertain terms, that those gifts didn't mean anything. All he wanted was some Dad time. Remember that big old alarm clock going off?

My goals and visions are clearer now than ever before, only now I am living for today. I have learned to appreciate what today has given me. Today is the present, and that is just what it is, a "present." Another word for present is "gift." The Bible says in Matthew 6:34, "Don't worry about tomorrow. Tomorrow will worry about itself. Each day has enough trouble of its own." I feel that this is only part of the picture for my life. It should also say, "Forget about yesterday's failures (take the lesson though), let go of the pain of past problems."

Among the lessons I learned from my business mentor and close friend Robert Harder was a gold nugget of advice that I have been able to apply regardless of my circumstances or season in life. He taught me that it is okay to fail, but, "Don't make a mistake on a mistake." Building on that, Brian Tracy taught me, "There is no such thing as failure, only feedback." If you take nothing else away from this small window into my life, just remember that if life is a superhighway, it is okay to spend some time on the shoulder, taking in the view.

Paul Usher

LIVING WITHOUT LIMITS

Brian Tracy

The starting point of great success and achievement has always been the same. It begins with you dreaming big dreams. There is nothing more important and nothing that works faster than casting off your own limitations so you can begin fantasizing about the wonderful things that you can become, have and do.

A wise man once said, "You must dream big dreams, for only big dreams have the power to move the minds of men." When you begin to dream big dreams, your levels of self-esteem and self-confidence will rise immediately. You will feel more powerfully about yourself and your ability to deal with what happens to you. The reason so many people accomplish so little is because they never allow themselves to lean back and imagine the kind of life that is possible for them.

A powerful principle you can use to dream big and live without limits is contained in what Elihu Goldratt calls the "Theory of Constraints." This is one of the greatest breakthroughs in modern thinking. What Goldratt has found is that in every process and in accomplishing any goal, there is a bottleneck or choke cord that serves as a constraint on the process. This constraint then sets the speed at which you can achieve any particular goal.

What Goldratt found is that if you concentrate all of your creative energies and attention on alleviating the constraint, you can speed up the process faster than by doing any other single thing.

Let me give you an example. Let us say that you want to double your income. What is the critical constraint or limiting factor that holds you back? Well, you know that your income is a direct reward for the quality and quantity of the services you render to your world. Whatever field you are in, if you want to double your income, you simply have to double the quality and quantity of what you do for that income or you have to change activities and occupations so that what you are doing is worth twice as much. You must always ask yourself, "What is the critical constraint that holds me back or sets the speed on how fast I can double my income?"

A friend of mine is one of the highest paid commissioned professionals in the United States. One of his goals was to double his income over three to five years. He applied the 80/20 rule to his client base. He found that 20 percent of his clients contributed 80 percent of his profits and that the amount of time spent on a high-profit client was pretty much the same amount of time spent on a low-profit client. In other words, he was dividing his time equally over the number of tasks that he does while only 20 percent of those items contributed to 80 percent of his results.

So he drew a line on his list of clients under those who represented the top 20 percent and then called in other professionals in his industry and very carefully, politely and strategically handed off the 80 percent of his clients that only represented 20 percent of his business. He then put together a profile of his top clients and began looking in the marketplace exclusively for the client who fit the profile. In other words, he looked for one who could become a major profit contributor to his organization. He chose those he in turn could serve with the level of excellence that his clients were accustomed to. Instead of doubling his income in three to five years, he doubled it in the first year!

So, what is holding you back? Is it your level of education or level of skill? Is it your current occupation or job? Is it your current environment or level of health? Is it the situation you are in today? What is setting the speed for achieving your goal? Remember that whatever you have learned, you can unlearn. Whatever situation you find yourself in, you can probably get yourself out of. If your real goal is to dream big dreams and live without limits, you can set this as your standard and compare everything that you do against it.

The three keys to living without limits have always been the same. They are clarity, competence and concentration. Clarity means you are absolutely clear about who you are, what you want and where you're going. You write down your goals and make plans to accomplish them. You set very careful priorities and you do something every day to move you toward those goals. The more progress you make toward accomplishing things that are important to you, the greater self-confidence you have and the more convinced you become that there are no limits to what you can achieve.

Competence means that you begin to become exceptionally good in the key areas of your chosen field. You apply the 80/20 rule to everything you do and you focus on becoming outstanding in the 20 percent of the tasks that contribute to 80 percent of your results. You dedicate yourself to continuous learning. You never stop growing. You realize that excellence is a moving target and you commit yourself to doing something every day that enables you to become better and better in your field.

Concentration is having the self-discipline to force yourself to concentrate single-mindedly on one thing, the most important thing, and to stay with it until it's complete.

The two key words for success have always been focus and concentration. Focus is knowing exactly what you want to be, have and do. Concentration is persevering, without diversion or distraction, in a straight line toward accomplishing the things that can make a real difference in your life.

When you allow yourself to begin to dream big dreams, creatively abandon the activities that are taking up too much of your time and focus your inward energies on alleviating your main constraints, you start to feel an incredible sense of power and confidence. As you focus on doing what you love to do and becoming excellent in those few areas that can make a real difference in your life, you will begin to think in terms of possibilities rather than impossibilities. You will move ever closer toward the realization of your full potential.

Brian Tracy

WAKE UP TO BE IN THE MOMENT
Linda S. Hines

Happiness requires being in the moment. I've spent many years of my life in the "then and when" instead of the "here and now." Living in the present moment is where happiness is. It is not in the past, because the past is just memories. It is not in the future, because the future is just a dream. I had to "wake up," let go of the past, let go of my fear of the future and begin to live my true purpose in life right now! I could only do that by being in the moment.

I had a guide once say to me, "All healing is a release of fear, and if you want to live life, say 'yes' more often." However, waking up and saying "yes" to life requires being in the present moment. In that moment, I felt mostly fear. In my fear, I couldn't breathe deeply; I couldn't think clearly. I felt alone. Fear kept me in a contracted state, where being in the moment and loving life was difficult, and for some, impossible.

Fear causes us to forget who we really are. Fear keeps us focused on the future. Fear lowers our vital life force energy, our vibration. Living from this lower state impacts our consciousness. In this lower state of consciousness, some might say, "Life doesn't seem worth living."

As a counselor, I am often asked, "Is it necessary to rehash the past and know why? I don't want to feel all those painful feelings again." In my experience, it is important to make connections between the past and the present, because the present is being colored by those unprocessed feelings from the past. Our vital life force is robbed from us when our energy is spent avoiding old, uncomfortable feelings or being stuck in them, letting them linger for hours, days or years. Why would we want to be in the moment when the moment is pain-filled? However, normal feelings have a beginning, a middle, and an end, and they are life-giving.

I believe my fear came from all the moving my family did while I was growing up. My dad worked pipeline construction and we moved wherever his job took him. My parents and I sat down some years ago to count the number of moves we had made and the number of cities, states and countries we had lived in before I completed high school. It was hard for them to do this. They both said, "There are a lot of things I just don't want to remember about those times." This process and our combined memories were a help for me. Fear makes you forget a lot of things. To sum it up, we had moved four or five times every school year for a total of 48 moves. We had lived in 21 states and three different countries before I graduated from high school, and my traveling didn't stop at high school graduation. After college, I married a man in the military and we moved for the next 18 years, living for nine years in Germany. I've now lived in Oklahoma for the past 23 years with my husband and children. The process of "being in the moment" is my life now.

Being in the moment also means becoming consciously aware and learning to listen to that deep part of self that I call "inner knowing." One day, while living in Germany, I was standing at the kitchen window, sad and depressed even though I had two beautiful children and a wonderful husband. I questioned my purpose for being on this earth. Is this all there is? There must be more to life than this! What on earth am I or any of us here for? I heard the answer in my own mind: "To help others get through the pain of being on this earth." At that time, I was not doing my life's work—I was too scared. Since the age of 12, when I lived in Tripoli, Libya, and read a magazine article about a psychiatrist working with emotionally disturbed children, I knew I wanted to work in mental health. Yet, I didn't believe I was smart enough to get a medical degree, a Ph.D., or a master's degree. Two beliefs—"I'm not smart enough" and "I'm too shy"—severely limited me. So, 10 years into a wonderful marriage and wonderful life, I was depressed. That day, 28 years ago, I made a deal with myself to go back to school even if I was scared. The next day, I enrolled in graduate school. At that time, I still didn't have a belief in Spirit, but Spirit was there, guiding me.

Even in my fear, I graduated on the dean's list from Boston University, and eventually owned a counseling business. As a counselor, I've had many life-changing experiences, including three years of intensive healing work in Heart-Centered Hypnotherapy and five years of training in Bioenergetics Analysis, a form of body therapy that absolutely requires you to be "in your body and aware at this moment."

I am certified as a Perfect Health instructor from the Chopra Center. I've walked on fire, attended Native American sweat lodges and been on a vision quest. Let me say, Neale Donald Walsch is not the only one to have had *Conversations with God*. As part of our fire walk ceremony, we had to discuss our fears. If we didn't have fear, we couldn't go down to the fire. You ought to attest to have fear of walking on hot coals! Our instructions were to ask our "inner knowing" if we could walk, listen for the answer and follow the directions. We circled the fire but no one walked. I said to myself, "Someone has to go first. I will." I headed toward the fire, then remembered I hadn't asked Spirit. I got back in the circle and asked, "Can I walk the fire?" Immediately the answer came, "Yes!" and just as quickly I asked, "But will I get burned?" The answer was: "Haven't I carried you many times?" I walked the hot coals and two-thirds of the way across, my toe went deep into the coals. It was hot and I thought, "My God, I'm burned!" I finished the walk, pressed my toe into the grass and realized my toe was not burned! Immediately, the answer came, "That's right, but if you had continued to tell yourself that it was burned, I would have given you what you were asking for."

The process of "being in the moment" results in facing our fears and releasing our resentments. This process releases the hold of the past and the future. You begin to wake up, become consciously aware, and develop a relationship with your "inner knowing" (that small guiding voice within). You understand everything has a beginning, a middle and an end. There is no happiness in the "then" or the "when." There is only happiness in the "now," in this moment. There is an unlimited amount of love that makes being in this moment the only place I want to be. You can "Live the Life You Love." I am!

Linda S. Hines

FORGET YESTERDAY, EMBRACE TODAY
Staff Sergeant S.R. Rosen

Several months ago, I was driving with my wife and two little boys on a beautiful Monday afternoon. I noticed the traffic ahead had halted along the small two-lane highway and I could tell there was an accident. Two large gravel trucks were lying on their sides and several people were guiding traffic and clearing away tires strewn on the road. I pulled over and got out to see if anyone needed medical attention.

Having been in the army, I knew some first aid. I figured I could help out if needed. I asked if anyone needed attention and was pointed to the front of one of the trucks that was wrecked on the road. There lay a man, face down, trapped in a mangled mess of steel. I was stunned. I had never seen anyone seriously injured, and it was obvious the man was. Someone said he was still alive, but I felt so helpless. There was nothing I could immediately do. Within minutes, the police arrived and I was asked to leave.

When I stepped back into my van, it was obvious I was extremely upset over what I had just seen. I had the feeling the man was not going to survive. I did not give my wife any details. As I pulled away, a thought crossed my mind, "If that was me, face down with my life fading, what would really matter? The price of gas? How well I did on a video game? How much money was in my bank account? Resentment for someone who had angered me? Hardly." I would have been thinking about my wonderful wife and my two precious boys. I felt my heart flood with the realization that if it had been me, I would have been full of regret and sadness. I considered the many times I ignored my kids to sit on the computer, or when I had not paid attention to my wife when she needed someone to talk to. I thought of how many days I had missed out on truly living by spending my energy on the past.

That night, I sat down and began typing my feelings. I had wanted to start a book about self-improvement for a while, but never had the motivation to start. I typed away, letting my emotions flow from my fingers to the keyboard. I was deeply moved by the accident and vowed to myself that I would change how I lived. I would make the most of each day and spend more time with my family. I was a changed man, and the old, apathetic version of myself was gone.

Tonight is the first time I have read the words I wrote on that life-changing day. I called the document "Wake Up!" How ironic that the title of the book you are reading begins, "Wake Up..." When I typed those words four months ago, I had never heard of the *Wake Up...Live the Life You Love* series. It's amazing how life works.

I am doing more with my wife and kids now and am making the commitment to change, but each day I find myself drifting back to old habits. How do I translate my words into consistent action? How can I make the most of each and every day?

Perhaps the answer to all of those questions is another series of questions. What good could possibly come from bringing up yesterday's failures? Will ruining today with thoughts of missed opportunities, regrets and guilt make me a better man? Of course not. It's just an old habit that is about as useful as ice fishing lessons in Jamaica. Part of enjoying today is to learn from yesterday, cherish the good memories and move on. This perspective gives me back some of today, but then comes the big challenge—the future!

I have yet to discover a way to predict the future, but that does not stop me from trying. It is one thing to plan for tomorrow, but it is quite another to create a muddy, negative version of it. I find that many of my negative feelings are a direct reflection of my irrational fears, concerns and anxieties about the future. I also find that my comfort and peace of mind are a direct reflection of positive expectations about the future. Tomorrow will come regardless of how I think and feel, so why on earth should I waste a single second of now on negative thoughts of the future? It is senseless.

If I have made peace with the past and done all I can to prepare for and make tomorrow better, it stands to reason that I am now free to explore and maximize the present. I can make the time to really enjoy my surroundings without being bombarded with yesterday's junk and tomorrow's unknown. When I actually take the time to stop and focus on the moment, I can focus on what really matters.

I find myself able to give 100 percent of my attention to my four-year-old son when he talks to me. I have time to enjoy tickling my 18-month-old and listening to him giggle. I can be goofy and find new ways to make my wife laugh excitedly. When I am living in the moment, I am better suited to be there for my family. Every time I am tangled in worries about the past or future, I am robbing the present of its value.

Living in the now is something about which I am certainly no expert. I just know it is the only way to live life to the fullest. As each day comes and goes, I am confident I will become better at creating a life I could have only dreamed of when I was younger. Each day is limitless in what it can offer. The only way to ensure I get the most out of each day is to take advantage of every moment.

This story is dedicated to Richard "Bill" Johnson:
July 9, 1949—May 12, 2008.

Staff Sergeant S.R. Rosen

SUCCESS THROUGH FAITH
Edward J. Sessa

How do you define success? You cannot work toward being successful unless you have an idea of what it means to you. I have found that success means different things to different people. Your goals may be related to work, family, health or your personal or spiritual life. I will help you define success and guide you to establish the goals you wish to achieve.

Success is not a destination, but a continuing day-by-day process that begins now. You can't change yesterday and tomorrow isn't here yet, so focus on what you can accomplish today. By *living in the now* you will enjoy the success that accompanies change. Many years ago, I learned the definition of success from a man much wiser than I. The definition he gave me was, "Success is the progressive realization of a worthy ideal" (Earl Nightingale).

Let's look at the three steps to success that will ensure you will reach your goals.

First, you must set a goal you believe you can achieve. If goal-setting is new for you, you should make sure the goal is realistic and that it can be accomplished in a short period of time. By doing this, you will gain confidence in the knowledge that you now have a method to reach your goals. Begin today and believe that you can reach those goals.

Second, you must create a plan of action. You have established a goal and now you need to decide what tasks you need to perform daily in order to reach your goal. Write them down and refer to them each day until you achieve your goal.

Third, you need to have the discipline to complete those tasks each day. As soon as you start working toward your goal, you will feel successful at your accomplishment. You must stay committed to the daily completion of the task. Remember, today is the only day you can affect change in your life.

When you achieve your first goal, you will begin to feel satisfaction. At this point, you may want to pick a different goal to work toward, or you may, based on your situation, refine your current goal and continue to work on it. Once you become comfortable with these principles, you can apply them to all areas of your life. Generally, most successful people are working toward several goals at once. Just decide what areas of your life you want to change and take it one day at a time.

Now that you have basic steps to become more successful and the tools to implement changes into your life, I am going to share with you the secret to maximizing your results. With this secret, you can reach your goals in a manner far beyond your expectations. The one essential thing to enjoying all the benefits of your success is faith. You may be asking, "How does faith come into play in reaching my goals and becoming successful?" "Faith" has many definitions. In this context, I would like to discuss faith as it applies to each of us individually and how faith in God can help us change our lives beyond our wildest dreams.

Faith in yourself could be described as the *sincerity of intentions*. As you set goals and decide upon tasks to achieve those goals, you are displaying faith in yourself that you will continue to perform the tasks.

Some of us may need a little more help in the area of faith, especially when we feel we are doing everything possible and are still failing to reach our goals. However, don't think faith in itself is the answer. Faith in God, incorporated with meaningful tasks, will produce results far beyond your imagination.

Let me give you an example of how faith in God totally changed my life. Most of my life, I have been very fortunate, setting my goals and reaching them in an appropriate time frame. I had several careers in the areas of sales, management and self-employment. I felt successful, but erroneously believed my success was all my own doing. At this point in my life, I had been self-employed for 20 years. I sold my business and began my search for the next venture. I spent six months working daily toward my goal of finding a new industry, but I simply couldn't find the right one.

At that point, I became somewhat frustrated and decided to ask for help. I prayed to God to allow me to find one last business to take me to retirement. I prayed daily, searching for the right business, and trusted God to direct me. In my prayers I told God I would do whatever He chose for me. I then found myself going back and analyzing a project I had ruled out months earlier. It was a security alarm business that now appeared to be perfect for me.

I filled out an application and was granted a dealership with the top company in the industry. From that day forward, I continued to pray for guidance and direction in running the business and my prayers were answered. I thought we would build a nice, small, one-office business with no more than 12 employees. We eventually opened five locations in three states, and as a result of my faith, we became one of the top dealers in the country. We were prosperous beyond my wildest dreams. To be sure, I set goals and implemented the tasks, but the guidance I received to make these decisions was pure inspiration. I had faith that I would receive direction from God to make the proper business decisions for my company. In 2007, God showed me what the next chapter in my life would be and provided a buyer for my business.

Now you know the secret to becoming a success. Set your goals, work toward them daily and have faith God will provide the guidance you need.

What's next for me? Well, that's easy. Ten years ago, when I asked God to lead me in my new business, I promised Him I would share with others how, with His help, I was able to flourish. I now consult with small businesses and bring the principles of success to their organizations. May God be with you.

Edward J. Sessa

THROWING OUT THE TUBE
Ernie Hudson

I graduated from high school, but not the same way or with the same sense of joy and accomplishment that many people share.

My grandmother raised me and I was told to get a high school education, which I did. However, she never said anything about my grades; I graduated with a D average. Then, to make the road to the future even bumpier, I got married at 18. My wife got pregnant right away, and suddenly, one day, it hit me: This was my life. I was working in a factory and I just felt trapped; I had no way out. I thought, "Maybe I'll go to college." But when I tried to get into college, that D average came into play. I couldn't get accepted anywhere.

One night, I just prayed over the whole mess that my life had become. Finally, I drifted off into sleep. I woke up around three in the morning, and I heard a voice saying, "Go downstairs and take the tube out of the TV." You may not believe it, but I did just what I had been told. Of course, when I took the tube out of the TV, my wife thought it was broken. With no TV in the evening, we had to fall back on simple conversation.

For the first time in our married lives, we started to really talk to each other. I found out that my wife was a great reader; she had a deep interest in people and in the world around her, and had the same kind of aspirations that I held in my heart. Well, we just turned our lives around. She was in the ninth grade when we got married; yet she went on to get her Ph.D. I finally got into college at Wayne State, then got a scholarship to Yale, and then I attended the University of Minnesota. On stage or screen, I've been doing what I love to do ever since.

I can never forget that there was one moment when I just *knew* I had to make a change in things. It was a moment of knowing, "I know there's another way, and I'm not seeing it." Sometimes you just have to ask for help. My life has never been—and never will be—the same. I literally woke up.

We watched so much TV those first months we were married; yet I couldn't remember what we watched the night before. Once we started to really communicate with each other, we realized that we both had dreams—a vision of what we wanted to do, and what we wanted to achieve in life. At that moment, we began to climb out of the hole we had gotten ourselves into.

What's your dream? Young people are often told to forget their dreams and prepare for a life of practicality. Acting or any career in theatre, they are told, is impractical. Well, if you really want to act, I say, "Do what you want to do." I talk to people every day who say they want to be an actor, but they only want to be in movies, to be seen on TV, and to be recognized as a celebrity. There is so much more to living a dream.

I discovered acting in college. College is a great place to really under-stand your craft; to learn what acting is all about. It's not about becom-ing rich and famous; it's about learning a craft and being able to do for a lifetime. I've been doing it for 40 years, and that's what it's about. To really live the life you love, and to live it with meaning, you may have to change your priorities and your goals. It's not about all the pretended glamour and celebrity, because those things really don't matter at the end of the day.

I have four sons: My two younger boys are in college and my two older sons have graduated from college. They have gotten their advanced degrees. I am so happy for them because they have laid the foundation for living a good life; a decent life. No matter what your career path, the same warning holds true: If you are looking for the glamour, the fame and the recognition, you are searching for an empty treasure chest. You are on the road to a very dead end.

So I would say you should lay out a strong foundation, because that foundation is what is going to carry you over the years. In spite of a few moments of possible glory, you don't really want to end up like so many friends I have known who are angry and bitter and disappointed because they were unfavorably compared to somebody else or they didn't quite get what they thought they wanted.

Reality is this: Find your craft, study, and train. Follow your dream, but never forget: Before you can follow a dream, you have to wake up.

Ernie Hudson

LESSONS FROM PARADISE:
A STEP OFF THE BEATEN PATH
Sam Chillingworth

I used to think I had life's rat race figured out: Study hard, get a good job, get married, buy a home, start a family, work my way up the corporate ladder and plan for retirement. Just check the boxes as you accomplish the tasks. Not much rocket science happening here—or so I thought.

At 22, I had landed a good job with a major pharmaceutical company and a ticket home to Hawaii. Within months of returning home, my college sweetheart moved from California to take our four-year relationship to the next level. Within a few years we were married and had purchased our first home, as the annual promotions continued to come in. By the time I was 26, I had closely followed the societal road map for success. I had studied hard, had the job, the girl, the house and the promotions and had handled the growing responsibility each new step brought to the table.

From the outside, it looked like I was headed down the highway to success at an amazing speed. My wife, whom I had met at 18 only weeks after arriving to college, was my best friend. We had watched each other grow up in the most identifying years of our lives, and we seemed like the perfect couple, but on the inside, I knew I was not living the life I was meant to live. I struggled for purpose and meaning, and fought with my own insecurities of not having enough money to provide the life to which she had grown accustomed. I questioned the long-term security of my employment and my fears grew larger as our standard of living rose in equal proportion to any increase in income. I had convinced myself that everything less than ideal in my life could be remedied by just getting over the next hurdle. The future was always the answer. "Sit tight," people would say. "Put your nose to the grindstone, and someday you'll wind up happy and successful."

"That's living?" I thought. I wanted more.

Looking for answers everywhere but inside myself, I found comfort in a relationship with a female co-worker almost 11 years my senior. She was understanding and nurturing and listened intently to my concerns for the future. More importantly, she possessed a spiritual nature within her that was intoxicating to be around. She encouraged me not to get lost looking anywhere but *inside myself* for the answers to the toughest questions about life, love and the pursuit of happiness.

Just like a scene from the movies, the relationship was exposed shortly after it began and months of scandal ensued, leaving many people surrounding us saddened, angry and confused. Those close to me couldn't believe my marriage had problems and my actions caught them by surprise. Furthermore, the thought of me with a woman 11 years older was almost too much for some to digest. Friends became enemies overnight. Family members were riddled with guilt and disappointment. My wife left me, the house was sold and I lost nearly 20 pounds in 30 days. All my successes were gone in a period of just a few months.

Yet, this is where it all began for me. I had been broken to the core and it was time to rebuild—one day at a time. For the first time in my life, "tomorrow" seemed too far away and the past too painful to continue visiting, so the present was the only safe place to be.

The rebuilding began very simply: with gratitude. Surviving day to day was much less painful when I began appreciating the fact that I still lived in one of the most beautiful places in the world. It started with a commitment to never miss the sun setting into the ocean every evening. I would be there no matter what I was doing, even if all I saw was the final moment. If not at any other time during the day, I made it a point to be present for those short moments, sharing in God's creation and realizing how many things happen day after day without the aid of mankind. Birds sing every morning, the stars continue to shine, my heart beats and my lungs continue to supply my body with oxygen, with or without my acknowledgment. It taught me that all of life has a purpose and that nothing we endure is by chance. While I wished I had made different choices with regard to the way I brought about the end of my marriage and past life, I believed in my soul it was all for a greater purpose. Thankful for that greater purpose, my gratitude was literally all I had to give. At the time, it was not a conscious spiritual move on my behalf, but rather a feeling that would lead me to take the first steps toward discovering who would emerge from the rubble of my past.

Giving thanks cannot be done at any other moment but the present. The more time I spent in the *here and now*, the more I realized that it is in this place that you are closest to the creation of all things. God, divinity, energy, love—whatever you choose to call the unknown force of creation—is found here. This is where the ego has the weakest foothold on your thoughts, allowing the unveiling of your true self. It is where the illusions of the past and future do not cloud your mind, leaving you open to inspiration, happiness, purpose and love. In short, it is life.

It is in the present that I realized I really knew nothing at all about the world except the energy within me. Not the "me" that your family, profession, socioeconomic status, gender, race or friends had pigeonholed me into, but the true life force within myself. The me that shows itself when my body tingles with joy when I do or say something that is in alignment with my inner self, granting me the only validation needed to confirm I am indeed on my path. It was here that I found my place in the world.

A commitment to living a thankful life has done wonders for me, as it will do for you. It is the first step among many to living the life you always wanted. It has allowed me to travel to more than 15 different countries, experience adrenaline-filled adventures that would blow your mind and brought me the forgiveness, happiness and love I'd once longed to receive.

If you are reading this, you have already made the commitment to taking the road less traveled. No matter who you are or what situation you are in, you are now ready. If you truly want to make a change in your life, take the first step, give thanks and be here *now*.

If you ever need support or encouragement, or want to learn more about living to your greatest potential, please contact me and I will be more than willing to help. Best of luck and remember: You can control your destiny.

Sam Chillingworth

RIGHT HERE, RIGHT NOW
Madisen Harper

For a good part of my life, I have been running an endless race and I have never made it to the finish line. As the end neared, I would set a new goal and the race would start all over again. I had turned into a human "doing" instead of a human "being" and all that striving without acknowledgement was exhausting. There was no victory lap or celebration for what I had achieved.

My desperate desire to escape the rat race meant I was focused only on the future, from the next holiday to the new job that was finally going to make me happy. Sadly, I never enjoyed what I currently had and living in the here and now was a concept that constantly eluded me, leaving me in a state of perpetual unease.

Work was the primary cause of my discontent, and for as long as I can remember, I always wanted out of the corporate world. Although I was highly ambitious in my marketing career, I didn't enjoy the game playing, politicking or trading time for money. The company and my values were simply misaligned.

After being "institutionalized" for 10 years, I woke up and refused to settle for anything less than work that fulfilled my heart. I resigned from my job and its six-figure salary and started a fashion business. Suddenly, I no longer lived for the future because the present was so much fun. I enjoyed the freedom, creativity and positive environment.

The name of the business was "2 Roads Design," inspired by Robert Frost's poem "The Road Not Taken."

> *Two roads diverged in a wood, and I—*
> *I took the one less traveled by,*
> *And that has made all the difference.*

A factor that had contributed to my unhappiness in the past was the tribal mentality that "we've always done it that way," "we don't want to rock the boat," and looking for problems instead of solutions. I was craving the road less traveled.

From time to time, naysayers would attempt to burst my blissful bubble with, "Why don't you get a full-time job?" and, "You'll never succeed. It's too hard to make money in fashion." It took me a while to realize that when "success strippers" said I couldn't do something, it was because they were unable to do it. Their comments had nothing to do with my abilities and everything to do with their level of confidence if they were to find themselves in the same situation.

Instead, I chose to focus on the "power of one," seeking to validate the possibility of success. If he or she could do it, so could I. I also surrounded myself with people who pulled me up instead of pushing me down.

After three semi-successful years, the company had not achieved the financial success I'd hoped for and the business was sold. I had been forced to refocus my career, but often found myself living in the past and commiserating the 2 Roads "failure." I was again living in a joyless existence.

In retrospect, I realized I had a narrow definition of success, and as time passed, I found 2 Roads' gift to me. It uncovered my passion for communicating. What price can you put on discovering your purpose? At its height, the business received millions of dollars in media coverage and I successfully promoted our message of positive body image and self-esteem. I was a sought-after spokesperson, was featured in dozens of publications and conducted motivating seminars. I consistently received feedback that I was inspirational and energizing.

Despite my revelation, I reluctantly left my dream behind as I caved to financial pressures and went back to being a marketing consultant.

My return to the corporate world reminded me of why I left, as I was surrounded by hundreds of employees who were miserable in their jobs and counting down the minutes until 5 p.m., the weekend, the next paycheck or the upcoming vacation. The average employee works 90,000 hours in his or her lifetime and spends a majority of that time resisting his or her unpalatable present. I was working with the "walking numb," people existing on life's baseline.

Neale Donald Walsch's quote played in my mind: "How can you think of wasting a moment doing something for a living you don't like to do? What kind of a living is that? That is not a living, that is a dying!" My purpose became clear. All the suffering, resistance and unhappiness I created by working in jobs I didn't enjoy was the origin and answer to the question, "How can I serve?" I was a classic example of, "You teach best what you most need to learn."—Richard Bach

I discovered that what "resists persists," so I changed my negative *attitude* about going to work and realized it wasn't all that bad.

I changed my *behavior*, quit gossiping and playing office politics and became positively energized.

I also changed my *environment* by creating flexible work with clients who were aligned with my values.

Change and choice were the keys to workplace happiness.

I was then inspired to create a revolution of people who enjoyed their work, were capable of high performance, were on purpose, were able to have a laugh, were more than decent to one another and crafted the best 90,000 hours they could. Once again, the precious present proved to be my gift.

I gained confidence when I realized every previous job gave me the experience I needed to excel in helping people move from loathing to liking—sometimes even loving—their work.

If only I'd understood earlier how life teaches us, I could have reduced my struggle and wasteful worrying of what might (and rarely did) happen. I thought, "If I don't get this job, I'll fall behind on my mortgage. If the worst happens, I can always sell my apartment and live with my parents."

Eventually, I made the decision to refocus my energy toward solutions instead of worrying. I reframed my thinking and in the above example, I realized I didn't have a money problem, just an idea problem.

At other times, I became concerned with the "how." "How will I find a publisher?" I wrote. "How will I know what to talk about?" I mentored. The question of "how" can be crippling, but when I stayed open to opportunity, "how" eventually presented itself.

I recalled the story of the man in a flood who feared for his life and decided he would be safer if he climbed on his roof. He stood there praying, "Dear God, please save me." Moments later, a man in a boat cruised by and told the man to jump in. He replied, "I'm okay, God will save me." An hour later, a helicopter flew above and the pilot yelled, "Grab the rope and we'll pull you up." The man shouted, "No thanks, God is going to save me." Hours later the man drowned and arrived in heaven. He angrily asked God, "Why didn't you save me?" God replied, "I sent you a boat and helicopter."

Now I have a consciousness that awakens me to opportunities. If I hear myself saying, "what a coincidence," it's a sure sign that a boat or helicopter has just crossed my path. I would never "drown" because I know there are endless possibilities and choices I can make at any moment to create a new outcome.

Often, I would become frustrated when things didn't happen quickly, but I reminded myself that every past situation I had experienced came to fruition at the right time, not my time.

Although there were disappointments when situations didn't turn out the way I wanted, I eventually learned everything happens for a reason. I adopted a "this, or something better" attitude which allowed me to be detached from the outcome. I even rationalized how I could pursue future ambitions while staying in the moment. I simply planned, visualized, dreamed and took action in the present to create a wonderful future. It's comforting to know all is well in the perfect present.

Now I consistently take one step at a time, and before I know it, I have stepped into the end result. The race is over and I am ready to let life's celebration begin right here, right now. I am reminded of the quote, "Yesterday is history. Tomorrow is a mystery. Today is a gift. That's why it is called the present."

Madisen Harper

KEEP IT CURRENT
Gregory Scott Reid

People often ask me, "Are you living for the now?" I reply, "Heck no!"

I wish I could live for the now. I bet you do as well and that is why you are reading this book. The good news is that it looks like we are both working on it.

Imagine all the time we have wasted worrying about the past; imagine the moments lost because of our fear of the future. The funny thing is, it's been estimated that we spend 90 percent of our lives worrying about the 10 percent that will actually happen. How many times have we had imaginary, one-way conversations with ourselves that never come to fruition?

We think, "When I get there, they'll probably say this. I'll reply that. Then, they'll say, 'Oh yeah?'" You get the idea.

More often than not, when you arrive at your destination, everything appears fine and the dialogue you were planning goes right out the window.

Realizing this early on and knowing I am far from a specimen of purity, I decided to live my life with a simple motto that has made my personal development journey an easier path to follow. My motto is about progress, not perfection. We are not perfect creatures, yet we do have the capacity to evolve.

When I catch myself in a panic over yesterday or dreading the hours ahead, I simply remind my inner-voice to "keep it current." By this, I mean stay in the moment, or in the *now*.

This does not suggest that we should forget about our past experiences, but it does suggest that we not dwell on what has transpired in our past. Instead, we should use that information as knowledge, which is the form in which it is delivered.

People often spend a fortune to learn from the journeys of others, yet for some reason it is hard for us to grasp the fact that we already have great wisdom from what has transpired in our own existence as part of our own mortal quest.

Gregory Scott Reid

FINANCIAL FREEDOM
Jan Kocjancic

As I write this story, I have in mind all of you who are beginning, or intend to begin, your own business.

Why did I begin with business? The answer is short and simple: Only because I wanted to have financial freedom. I wholeheartedly believe this book will help you to attain financial freedom, as similar books have helped me.

The pivotal moment in my life was when I was 20 years old. A prestigious German football union league asked me to play for them. I wanted to be fit, so I went to a bodybuilder to ask him for diet advice. He asked me some questions regarding my nourishment. He asked, "What does your menu look like?" My answer was, "normal." Then he asked me, "What does 'normal' mean to you?"

This question made me think. I began to think more openly, and new horizons opened to me, which meant the world is not revolving around me. What is normal for me might be abnormal for someone else. I knew this before the question was asked, but this moment was different. Maybe the term "usual" is better than the term "normal." I sought out to find what is right, rather than what is normal. This question represented a turning point of comprehension for me—I began to understand other people and the world. I became more open to new ideas and new things. Since I became a sportsman, I have learned discipline and perseverance and have become accustomed to training. All this helps me now in my business.

The intellect, like a parachute, works only when it's open. An open mind is necessary for a good idea to fall on fertile soil. Some ideas helped me to attain the financial freedom and the vision to overcome the impediments in my way. The first idea was about passive and active income.

My business card reads:
"Do you work for money? >job,
Or does money (business) work for you?"

The result of the first line is little free time for what you would like to do and not enough money for what you would really like to have. The result of the second is freedom to make your own decisions about your schedule, itinerary and earnings.

Because of this idea, my perception of business changed completely. Passive income is the only way to attain financial and time freedoms.

The idea that had great influence on my income is "go to the best." Find the best people in your field of work. The idea which helped me to move is, "Don't wait for the ideal moment to work toward your goals." The ideal moment is now. I have learned in business that one good investment can be worth more than the income from your job. To be successful—whether in business, transforming your character or in flourishing relationships with fellow creatures—we have to gather the courage to overcome the obstacles inside ourselves! Only then can we reach our goals. The more calls you make, the more successful you become.

Though I didn't read much until I was 20 years old, I began to read a lot. Thank God I realized that successful people read a lot and their minds are open to new ideas. The third idea to help me reach financial success was to learn from the best. The only way to avoid criticism is to say nothing, to do nothing and to be nothing. One can only be free when he does what he purposed for himself and, most importantly, when he works on himself. One must change himself and the most important challenge is the victory.

For a person, like me, who likes to travel, there are only three things you need: time, money and health.

What is normal for you?

Jan Kocjancic

FREEDOM
Dr. Michael Beckwith

I free myself from the need to judge any person, nation or event. My consciousness is at peace, for it is now rooted and grounded in the Spirit. My thinking is premised on Infinite Mind, and I am established in love, compassion and forgiveness.

From the center of my heart, I radiate compassion to all beings, knowing that their pain is bathed in the Infinite Love of the Spirit.

I awaken the spirit of forgiveness within me. Even now it fills my consciousness with loving kindness towards myself with all beings. I judge not, lest I be judged. I love with the unconditional love of God.

Right here, right now, Divine Love loves through me. Divine Right Action frees me from the errors of human judgment and causes me to know that all beings are emanations of the One Life.

The true spiritual essence is all I know of each person. I think rightly, and I love greatly. I live to let love express itself through me.

I accept the fullness of life and am a distribution center of compassion, forgiveness, and love. I am blessed and prospered by Divine Love as it flows through me now.

I declare my faith in God and release material patterns of behavior. I know that God is at the center of life and I depend upon that which projected all creation as its own to be the source of eternal safety and security for all beings.

Dr. Michael Beckwith

Living In The Now

Allow It To Be Easy
Connie Russert, M.S.

Paularyo*, what are the benefits of living in the now, and how can we do that?

My dear, your question is one about the quality of life. Living in the pain of the past, and/or the fear of the future leads you out of the peace of the present.

What are the benefits of living in the now? Living in peace.

How? Imagine, if you will, a bubble of energy around your physical body.

My dear, this is your energy field. Allow yourself to imagine it, and then you will create within your bubble a safe and sacred space.

Okay, I can sort of see the bubble. Now what?

First, my dear, imagine your bubble is shrink-wrapped around your body. In an attempt to protect yourself from pain or fear, you often shrink your bubble. Do it now. How does it feel to your body to shrink-wrap your bubble? How does it feel to your mind? To your emotions?

I feel like I have a wet suit on. I'm tense and my mind is spinning.

When you shrink-wrap your bubble, you go to your head and live in the pain of the past and/or the fear of the future. You are acutely aware of your surroundings. You are on guard physically, mentally and emotionally. Your body becomes tense. Your mind becomes tense. Your emotions become tense. You enter the state of dis-ease.

Imagine now that you choose to allow it to be easy.

How? What do I do?

- Allow your energy field, your bubble, to expand to at least four feet from your body.
- Allow it to continue expanding as you:
- Insist that any energies or entities stemming from anything other than the highest Source of light and love leave your bubble immediately;
- Invite your spirit guides into your bubble;
- Invite in your angels;
- Invite in Jesus, Buddha, Mohammed...all the masters;
- Invite in the archangels;
- Invite in Mother Earth;
- Invite in the Source;
- Allow yourself to feel their presence, their love, their support;
- Invite in all the energies and entities from the highest Source of light and love to be with you and to bring you the energy and the information that is for your best and highest good, and for the highest good of all.

All right. Now what?

Notice that as your bubble continues to expand, your breathing is deeper. Your body is softer. Your mind is quieter and your emotions are calmer. Feel it. Be it. Enjoy it. Allow it to be easy.

My dear, now allow your bubble to double in size. Feel it. Be it. Enjoy it. Allow it to be easy.

Allow your bubble to double once more. Allow your bubble to continue expanding.

Allow it to be as large as is comfortable for you in this moment—perhaps as large as the universe and beyond. In this moment, feel how it is to be in your expanded bubble. Feel the presence of your guides, angels, masters, the archangels, Mother Earth, the Source, the energies and entities and information from the highest source of light and love. Float in these energies. Give yourself the gift of being in this moment. Allow it to be easy.

You have entered the peace of the present. Spend a few moments here. You are creating around you a safe, sacred and healing space. This is a healing moment for you. Allow it. Allow it to be easy.

Okay, it feels great! But how do I use this in my everyday life?

In this moment, be in your expanded bubble. Imagine extending out of your solar plexus a path. This is your life path. It extends in front of you, representing your future, and behind you, representing your past. For a moment, shrink your bubble. Now, imagine stepping onto your future path. Imagine it is tomorrow and you spend the day walking this path with your bubble shrink-wrapped. How do you feel physically, mentally and emotionally?

Tense. Tight. Rigid.

Come back to this moment. Allow your bubble to be as large as is comfortable for you, perhaps as large as All-That-Is. Allow it to be easy. Imagine stepping forward for a day in your expanded bubble. Imagine it is tomorrow and you spend the day in your expanded bubble. How do you feel physically, mentally and emotionally? How is your day different than the day you spent with your bubble constricted?

Easier. Lighter. Gentler.

The events in your day do not change. Your perception of the events changes. Your response to the people in your day changes. When you are in your expanded bubble, you see with compassion instead of judgment. When you are in your expanded bubble, your soul is free to come forward. When you are in your expanded bubble, you lead your life with your soul, instead of with the personality which lives in fear of the future or is stuck in the pain of the past. When you allow your bubble to expand, you feel "free to be me."

I love this!

When you allow your bubble to expand, you are the manifestation of your soul qualities.

What are my soul qualities?

In this moment, be in your expanded bubble. Feel it. Feel your energy in your expanded bubble. This is your soul's energy. This is the real you.

Say out loud:
I am loving;
I am compassionate;
I am peaceful;
I am joyful;
I am wise.

What are your other soul qualities? Say them out loud. Write them down. This is the you that is free, that creates a safe and sacred space within your bubble for your own healing and for the healing of others. This is the you that is here and now and allows it to be easy.

How can I stay here?

My dear, it is your choice. We wish for you to make a choice—in this moment—to allow it to be easy. Choose to allow your bubble to expand a zillion times a day until it becomes your new habit. Choose a piece of jewelry, a pen or something that is constant in your life. Each time you see this object, it will remind you to allow your bubble to expand. Choose to be free to be you. Choose to create a safe and sacred space for yourself and others. Choose to live from your heart and allow your soul to lead in order to be loving, compassionate, caring, wise and joyful. It is your choice.

> Choose to allow your bubble to expand.
> Embody your soul, your spiritual essence.
> Manifest your divine destiny.
> Allow it to be easy.

And it is so.

With blessings we wish you ease in every moment,
Paularyo

Connie Russert, M.S.

*Paularyo: This gentle (and often funny!) Council of seven Master Spirit Guides call themselves, collectively, Paularyo. They create a safe and sacred space within which Connie Russert, M.S., channels healing energy and practical tools from the highest Source of light and love. Paularyo reveal to you the kindest, gentlest *you* that is, and your elegant soul within. Paularyo come to help you overcome your life challenges and enhance your personal power. They share with you heart-based, soul-centered spiritual tools that you can use on a daily basis for ongoing transformation and healing toward self-empowerment.

COACHING GAVE ME MY LIFE BACK
Tony Husted

"Tony, pay attention!" requested my mother. "Tony, focus!" reminded my teacher. "Tony, stay on track!" commanded my father.

All of the responsible adults in my life—from my career military father to my stay-at-home mother to every teacher I had from grade school through high school—constantly reminded me to pay attention, but my brain literally had a will of its own.

I spent most of my childhood thinking about things like Matchbox® cars and *Star Wars*™ toys—anything but school. School was boring because I didn't know how any of it applied to my life. My rampant imagination was always someplace else—dreaming about fantasy worlds, about what I was going to do later in the day and about different movie scenarios.

Getting older didn't help. I just traded toys and fantasy worlds for reliving negative experiences or imagining the future. I was never in the now. The now was always occupied by thoughts of the future or the past.

After barely completing high school, I joined the U.S. Army and found my thoughts consumed by that experience. While I was at work, I was thinking about work and when I wasn't at work, I was thinking about not being at work. I constantly worried about what had been left undone or what I should have done differently. Like a security camera in the corner, I spent all of my time out of my body, looking at my own life.

Following the lead of the adults in my life, I did eventually learn to focus. The only problem was I always focused on being someplace else, on what was wrong or on what I didn't want. If I didn't want to fail the Army physical fitness test, my mind ran rampant for days about not failing the test. By the time I took the test, I was totally stressed out from focusing on not failing.

I cycled between floating off into dreamland to escape the stress and sinking into a state of constant worry about the negative past and how it might play out in the future. This created a vicious circle in my life that robbed me of enjoying what I was doing in the moment.

Later in life, I became a professional dancer. I fell in love with vintage swing dancing and spent five to seven nights a week dancing socially, practicing, taking classes or doing workshops. However, as much as I loved dancing, I still found myself somewhat detached. From my security camera view, I could see the experience, but I couldn't feel my body or emotions. I was disconnected from all of it.

Occasionally, dancing would startle me awake. Once in a while, I could feel the movement and experience the pleasure of being present in the moment. It was my first taste of turning off the camera in my mind and stepping into the flow. Then my real wake-up moment happened: I received an invitation to step into my life and start living it.

"Tony, just be in your body for a moment," suggested my life coach. "Take a moment and feel what you feel. Notice how it feels to think about this."

I was asked to simply be present in the moment in my own body. I wasn't asked to think about words or facts or content. I was asked to think about how I felt. I began to connect with the sensation of my body and the experience of the moment.

Life coaching introduced me to living in the now. I stopped focusing on the past and the future and started tuning in to what I wanted now and how that felt. I took the security camera off the wall and stepped fully into my life for the first time.

In training to be a life coach, I tuned in more and more to what I really wanted in my life. Then the realization hit me: In many ways, I already *had* what I wanted. I just wasn't experiencing it because I was so detached!

Up to that point, I had lived my life from the outside looking in, always evaluating, always worried I wasn't doing things well enough. Coaching showed me how to set that evaluation aside and simply live in the moment. I discovered there was no failure, simply feedback. If something didn't go the way I wanted in the moment, I could go back later, glean lessons from it and decide how I would do it differently the next time.

As I traded the failure viewpoint for the feedback lens, I found myself enjoying each moment even more. This set me free to fully step into the moment and live it. Obsessing about the future and the past faded into the wonderful reality of now.

It felt fabulous to just be present with my coaching clients in the moment—sitting, listening and focusing on them. I danced better as I focused completely on the movement and my partner. My relationships improved. Exercising changed. Previously, I had done everything I could to be out of my body, ignoring strenuous exercise and pain. Now, I reveled in the experience of working with my body, enjoying the pain and the progress. My health improved as I started to listen to my body. I received the aches and pains as feedback to help me make healthier decisions.

Even sleeping became easier. For years, I had struggled with insomnia. I used to lie in bed and think about all the things left undone and all the ways I had failed. I would think about all the things I should do the next day. Learning to live in the moment allowed me to just relax and feel my body lying on the bed under the covers. Now, I could briefly review the learnings from the day and just let tomorrow be tomorrow.

By learning to live in the now, I realized always focusing on the future caused me not to see what I already had. I was giving up the pleasures of this moment, of this day, for the hope of something more in another place and time. But when I stepped into the now of my life, I found I had many of the things I dreamed about for years—peace, joy, close relationships, security. I always thought I needed them on a vast scale, which was somehow out of my reach. Through living in the present, I realized these things *were* within my reach. They were already mine if I just slowed down and paid attention to what was going on around me, to the person talking, to what was going on inside of me.

I also found that when I slowed down, I got into quiet, peaceful moments where I was more open to hearing God. Looking back over my life, I saw all the times I ran frantically from one thing to the next, worrying about what would happen next, what people would think, what could go wrong, what I didn't want. I left God precious few opportunities to give me insight or guidance, to nudge me in one direction or another.

Now, I live my life fully awake and present. I focus on creating a life that allows me to be in the moment, in my body, to just be awake—living the life I love. When I take time to dream, I dream about the things I want more of in my life and how I might get them. When I pause and reflect on my past, I collect the strengths and lessons learned as feedback to guide how I want to do things in the future.

Now, I look around and see people with music playing, computers running and cell phones ringing. They never have a quiet moment to just listen, reflect and enjoy the moment. People are living with their eyes down and their ears closed. They aren't looking at the beautiful landscapes around them and seeing all the things that are possible. They aren't listening to themselves, to God or to one another. People are living an out-of-body experience, completely disconnected from reality, unaware of what is going on in the now.

Life coaching gave me my life back. By learning to live in the now and becoming very clear on what I love—being in the present with my clients—I get to live a life I love every day. I'm blessed to be a life coach, working with people to become more aware and more present, helping them wake up and live the life they love.

Tony Husted

THE GIFT OF BEING PRESENT
Colleen Walters & Laurie Fitzgerald

Laurie Fitzgerald, from Australia, and Colleen Walters, from Canada, are two very different women with two separate and amazing success stories with one common denominator: They each have unwavering self-belief with the will to succeed in business and in life. Their stories will inspire you to greatness.

Laurie has had a passion for sales since she was old enough to set up shop. Being raised in a small country town in a family that owned the only café, her first memories were of serving others. This gave her the desire to find a way to achieve financial freedom. Although her parents set a great example of work and ethics, they were from a very different generation. Having a secure job (just over broke) was their main concern for each of their children. Luckily, her passion to succeed was greater than the limiting holds of a so-called "real job." Laurie built a multi-million dollar direct sales business in less than four years and now enjoys financial freedom and the gift of living in the present. She enjoys each and every day she has on this amazing earth.

Colleen had just completed her enrollment forms for her M.B.A., when she was introduced to the direct sales business model. She made a quick decision to start the business and gain experience rather than studying business for four years to end up with an equivalent income. Colleen quickly built a multi-million dollar distributor business within four and a half years. She then moved into a worldwide corporate consulting and speaking role with a network marketing company. She utilized her skills in party planning to develop a unique system of selling and recruiting within the MLM model.

Who would have thought two very different women from two very different countries would be united in Australia with the common purpose of empowering women to dream, believe and achieve? Their definition of success is to continue to strive to reach your destination no matter how many challenges you may encounter along the way. Success lies within the journey. The present is in the journey; the destination is in the future. These women hold the following quote dear to their vision: *"The future is not some place we are going to, but one we are creating. The paths are not to be found, but made, and the activity of making them changes both the maker and the destination."* —John Schaar

Their common denominator was an unwavering belief in the abilities each of their parents instilled in them. They were taught early on in life that they could achieve anything on which they set their minds. Neither of them ever lost that belief, no matter what difficulties or challenges life presented them. They picked themselves up, dusted themselves off and put their heads down and bums up and kept working toward the goal. Focus and determination kept them on track.

Across the globe, during the same period of their lives, they competed in many team and individual sports throughout their teenage and young adult lives. Having this background fine-tuned their skills of being present and focused for extended periods of time. Not only did they have minute, hourly and daily presence and focus, but also the ability to focus on long-term visions and goals, which kept them in line to achieve their individual goals. This skill enabled them to learn the discipline necessary for success in life and business.

Being present means being in the moment with a clear sense of what is going on around you and participating in it. It takes practice, we have learned. However, it is paramount to success in business and in life not to live in the future or past, but to be present today so that no current opportunities are missed. A clear vision of the future goal is also essential in continuing to build momentum. Understanding or objectively evaluating the past ensures you do not waste time revisiting prior learning experiences. To stop altogether—to be stuck in the past, present or future—stops momentum, so a balanced approach is critical to your success.

When you are present, you can enjoy your environment, connect with the people around you and be aware of everything. This presence enables a process replenishment of your energy so creative thoughts can flow more easily. When we are too busy with the stress of the future or the pain of the past, we stop the creative flow of the present. Have you ever noticed creative ideas flow when we stop? Just think of the busy season in your life or business when you are in survival mode. Each time you stop and take a break, have you noticed that all of a sudden incredible, creative ideas just flow? This is the gift of the present!

Giving the gift of your complete presence to the people around you shows how much you value and truly care about them. Think about the most rewarding moments in your life. They aren't conversations or events you can't completely recall. They are moments you can clearly see and describe in detail and in which you can feel the emotions as though they happened yesterday. They are moments in which you were clearly and fully present and focused. You were not multi-tasking, distracted or stressed, but completely in the moment.

Both Laurie and Colleen had people in their circles of influence who did not hold the same beliefs about their goals and ambitions as they did. Laurie's personal struggle was the limiting belief of others that she should not earn a higher income than people who had studied for their career for many years. Colleen's personal struggle was the limiting belief of what other people thought of her goal to earn a six-figure income through direct sales, not through the completion of her M.B.A. These struggles were the result of other people's own self-limiting beliefs about worthiness, money and formal education.

If either one of them had let other people's personal beliefs override their own, they would not be where they are today, earning the incomes they desire and living the lifestyle of which many only dream. When they held their own personal beliefs strong that they could be, do, or have anything, they were in flow or rhythm, and events moved as they should. Again, the gift of presence, focus and determination helped them realize their dreams.

Laurie and Colleen agree that when they are clear and can focus on the end result while maintaining a presence in the here and now, they can achieve whatever their minds can conceive.

For Laurie, life is about inspiring others to dream big and truly gain what they want from life. This, in turn, fulfils her dream of inspiring others to have a champion attitude and champion belief in themselves.

For Colleen, life is about being in service to others; through that, her own dreams are realized, which inspires greatness! Now that she has realized her own potential, she can help others reach their visions and realize their own purposes through being fully present, completely focused and holding unwavering belief in themselves and their dreams.

Both Laurie and Colleen agree that they have influenced thousands of women and men alike to believe in themselves and to never put a ceiling on their potential. They have never asked others to do what they were not prepared to first do themselves.

If two cashiers can find a way to build two separate multi-million-dollar empires across the globe through simply believing in themselves and having the determination and the discipline to be fully present and accountable, then so can you!

Live in the moment and succeed!

Colleen Walters & Laurie Fitzgerald

LISTENING FOR GOD (FROM THE WAKE UP LIVE MOVIE)
Zachary Levi

My "Wake Up Moment" was when I realized how much God loved me, and that there were things in my life that I wanted to do and things I felt like God had made me do. He wasn't keeping things from me because he was mad at me, he was keeping them from me because he knew that I wasn't ready for them. When I realized that, and when I realized that he wanted to bless me with those things, and I was getting my life together, then it all started falling into place. And so, my "Wake Up Moment" was knowing God's love.

So, I would just tell young professionals of any kind to make sure you know why you want it. Is it because you really love the art of it, is it because you're really into the fame and the fortune? Know your motives as best you can, and know your passions as best as you can. If you are really passionate about it, you will go forward and succeed. You know, it's almost not even a choice.

So, it's not as if you're asking, "Should I be an actor?" It's "I have to be an actor, or a musician," or whatever the case may be.

But you also have to know that this may not be what you are ultimately supposed to do. Maybe it's just something you're supposed to pursue for a time that will bring you somewhere else. It should never be about who you are. It doesn't define you. You could go off to be the next Wolfgang Puck, but you never would have found that if you hadn't come to Hollywood and tried to be an actor. So, always be open to wherever God is taking you.

Zachary Levi

ARE YOU DANCING IN LIFE?
Denise Caiazzo

Just for a moment, close your eyes and take a deep breath. As you exhale, imagine yourself being gracefully whisked around a dance floor in perfect unison with your sexy, smiling partner, your body pulsating with the rhythm and your emotions elevated to a higher state of awareness. Are you sashaying across the floor in a waltz or stirring up your sensual side with a hot Latin number? Is that *you* on *Dancing with the Stars*? One thing is certain: You are completely alive—body, mind and soul—in this wondrous moment, brimming with verve and passion! You are living fully in the now!

How often do you have that feeling? Keep in mind I'm not talking about escaping into yesterday's memories or tomorrow's wishes, but rather, what are you aching to do, feel and be right now? Let's talk about how "being here, now" can unleash your passions, transform your life and set you on a solid path to living a life you love every single day.

I discovered early on that dancing fulfills me. There's something about feeling all of those sensations that is so freeing, so healing, so invigorating. The truth is, I can't imagine going even a few days without moving to life's beat. For me, the dance of life takes the form of actual dancing. What do *you* do that conjures up that same feeling of wholeness, connectedness and joy? What's your passion? What do you feel most alive doing? Is it martial arts, gardening, baking cakes, building model ships, arranging flowers, hiking, cycling, writing, traveling? Did a feeling, a thought or maybe a word instantly come to your awareness? There, that's it. What's the first thing that popped into your mind?

I know someone who said she didn't know when I asked, "What makes you happy, what's your joy?" She spent so much of her life taking care of her family (and everyone else who crossed her path) that she was completely out of touch with her own passions. She wasn't living in the moment at all. That happens all too frequently in this hyper-speed world of ours, filled with demands and pressures. If you're having some difficulty figuring this one out, here's another way to unearth what really moves you. Take another breath, exhale, and ask yourself, "What would I rather be doing right now more than *anything* else in the world?" Trust the answer that comes. Honor your intuition. If you're smiling, you've hit the nail squarely on the head.

The next question is, "Are you allowing yourself to express that passion *in some way* in your life?" As much as I love dance, I chose at a relatively young age not to become a professional dancer. I like "the good things" in life and decided to move into another line of work that would ensure I would achieve the lifestyle I wanted. It was the best choice. I rediscovered dance at a later stage in my life as a young adult living in New York City, and again more recently, when my ex-husband and I decided to separate. It was the right decision, so we both drummed up our courage and parted ways. A week later, I noticed a sign at a nearby club that said "Tito Puente's Orchestra: Salsa lessons at 8 p.m." I stepped onto the dance floor once again and that sense of joy and passion flooded back into my life at a time when I needed it most. I recalled all the benefits of living in the moment. To make a long story short, I'm now what some affectionately call a "salsa-holic." I have taught both salsa and belly-dancing as a side business and have had the great pleasure of performing. There's nothing so satisfying in life as doing something you love and seeing how it inspires others. It's interesting how life hand delivers extraordinary opportunities when we're on our perfect path and in touch with what moves us.

Maybe you've found your passion and have decided to pursue it in your spare time instead of attempting to make a career out of it. I'm here to tell you that it's okay. The *secret* to living a life you love is simply to be here now and passion it up! Turn up the volume by adding something that truly turns you on. Identify that one thing you'd rather be doing than anything else in life. Then, find a way to express it.

If you work from nine to five, Monday through Friday, in an office, but just love martial arts or yoga, then sign up for that class on Tuesday and Thursday evenings. If you're a stay-at-home mom or dad and you've always wanted to travel, start reading books about a place you want to visit. Make it a reality. If you've been meaning to sit down and play that piano again, just do it. Carve out the time, even if it's just one hour a week, to immerse yourself in that thing you love.

Here's what will happen. When you give yourself that gift, whether it's every day or even once a week, you experience life more fully and recharge yourself at all levels. Your heart begins to feel light and joyful. Your body thrives on the new sensation of living. Your spirit soars. You have new ideas, and solutions to problems begin to appear. You now have more energy, more focus, more *life*!

I just have one more question for you, "Are you 'dancing' in life?"

For some, dancing literally brings them into a heightened state of being. Really, it's a question of movement and what gets you excited. Life constantly changes and vibrates with energy, never remaining static. When I ask if you're dancing in life, what I really mean is, are you allowing yourself to move and be moved by what's happening in the present moment? What can you do differently today to live more fully in the now?

Denise Caiazzo

FAILURE AS A CATALYST
Victor Whitmore

Failure is the catalyst that breeds success. Know failure and success will know you. There is a quote I love and have clung to from the very moment I heard it eight years ago. It comes from Napoleon Hill, who said, "Every adversity, every failure, every heartache carries with it the seed of an equal or greater benefit."

Failure is not failure unless you give up. I believe failure is a part of being successful and moreover, it is necessary for achieving great things in this life. All great business leaders I have read about have experienced troubles and failures that would send most people to their graves. The reason they rose to the top is because failures sharpened, refined and strengthened them. A project or business idea may have gone bad or not worked, but they never viewed themselves as failures. On the contrary, they used those experiences to better themselves. When life put immense pressure on them, they pushed back and grew stronger, mightier and smarter. Those who don't live this way are the ones who never pass the test. They stay at the bottom and never figure it out. We simply cannot be promoted unless we pass the test at a particular stage in our lives.

I believe every situation that looks like failure, tragedy or hopelessness is actually an opportunity to shine and overcome. It's an opportunity to allow life to test you and make you better. It is a system, and in every system, there are rules. You cannot win the game unless you know the rules. Through every trial we face, we can learn a lot. There's no doubt that education is expensive. Go to Harvard or Yale's Web site. Call Stanford and ask how much tuition costs. Every failure is a great educational opportunity that will make you smarter and help you do better on the next project, business or investment. It may be costly, but a good always education is! With each new experience, you get a little smarter. Those who know this have an incredible advantage in life because they know what separates the achievers from the bottom feeders. A Harvard degree will get you a six-figure income. A business or real estate education will give you an unlimited income!

If you have tried and failed, I personally say, "Good for you." You took on a risk knowing it could take you down financially, but as my business partner Joel Thompson once said to me, "As life goes on, you're hardly ever regretful when you decide to do something—only when you decided not to." One of my mentors, Robert Kiyosaki, says, "If you're going to go down, take the bank with you. Don't fool around with duplexes!" Donald Trump has filed for bankruptcy twice on casinos he owns. The bank won't even talk to you if it is foreclosing on a few small rental homes, but let's see how hard everyone works on cleaning up a mess dealing with millions of dollars for you. Quite a different story! Who's in the driver's seat now? The ones who stepped out, faced fear straight on and took on more than they thought possible are the ones who stood tall and never gave up!

Good for you, I say. Keep on keeping on! Robert Kennedy said, "Only those who dare to fail greatly can ever achieve greatly." You know, if you're not failing every now and then, that's probably a good sign that you're not really doing anything. Victory comes only after many struggles and defeats. Each difficulty is an opportunity to move forward, to keep on keeping on and to determine to never give up. By turning away from your failures and avoiding them, you actually throw away your fortune. Napoleon Hill said, "Most great people have attained their greatest success just one step beyond their greatest failure." Whatever you do, do not give up. Don't let your pride get in the way because you are afraid of failure. Many people who have made the biggest mistakes have made the most money. Thomas Edison failed at 10,000 experiments when he was trying to invent the light bulb. Are you willing to fail 10,000 times before you find your dream?

People who don't understand that failure is part of becoming successful ultimately let their failures turn them into an overall failure. Those who do understand this principle allow their failures to propel them into success as they learn. They do not feel sorry for themselves about what has happened in the past. They do not allow regret to overtake them. To be a winner, you will certainly have to overcome failure, for it is in the course of such adversity that your willpower will be tried.

Remember that success is not partial to our needs. It is not partial to our circumstances or backgrounds. This system I refer to is moved by desire, not luck. It is moved by your willingness to stay the course, overcome the obstacles and hang in there when you want to quit. You must stick it out until the end and never give up! That is it! That is the key! That is the secret! There are no magic formulas to success. Are you willing to prevail? Ask yourself that question. Are you willing to prevail in the midst of defeat, in fire, despair, trials and tribulations? Are you willing to do whatever it takes to see your desire through to a successful end? If you can honestly answer yes, then you are well on your way to victory.

Understand today that failure is a prerequisite to your success. Your greatest achievement is one step past your greatest failure. Those who are willing to fail are those who are preparing themselves for glory, greatness and responsibility for the success that they will likely experience. Dale Carnegie said, "The person who goes farthest is generally the one who is willing to do and dare." Your success today is hiding in your greatest challenges. Step up to them, take charge and learn from them. You will find your dreams handed to you on a silver platter, wrapped in the finest silk and made with the purest gold. Dare to dream!

Victor Whitmore

MINDFUL MOMENTS
Lori Meadows

"I do not require of you to form great and serious consideration in your thinking. I require of you only to look."—Saint Teresa of Avila

When you stop and think about the power of a moment, it's amazing just how important they all really are. Try engaging in a moment with your mind open. In a split second, lives change, sometimes for the better and sometimes for worse. Babies are born and lives are lost. Relationships are formed and also broken. Think about the many times you have said something only to regret having said it.

It's very rare that we, as human beings, are consciously aware of our thoughts and are controlling our minds. As a matter of fact, these times are precious and few. Think about the times we arrive at a destination and don't even recall how we got there. We just traveled on autopilot with our minds racing a million miles an hour, thinking about everything but the moment in which we were living. Wouldn't life be much more fulfilling if we really engaged in our moments and made the most of our time?

So how do we gain control of our racing mind and maximize a life of abundance?

The power of listening and quieting the mind is first and foremost. God gave us two ears for this very reason. You need to stop scrambling through your mind for the perfect response and just engage in listening to the story or event unfolding before you. This simple task could be life-changing. It is easier said than done, but with perseverance and discipline, the magic of listening will unfold a whole new world before your eyes.

A simple step to begin this practice is to set a goal for your day. When you first wake up, simply put your feet on the floor and say, "Today I will use these ears to hear and refrain from using my tongue. I will count to 10 before responding in conversation so I fully take in the moment. I will listen without forming a judgment. God, please open my heart and help me to come from a place of peace and understanding."

Life is full of lessons, and by just applying this simple step, you can reduce repeating the same lessons. Time is something we all feel so tapped out of. You continually hear how human beings don't have the time to set a goal or to meditate for five minutes a day. My response is that you are absolutely correct: You don't have time. If you are not controlling your mind and setting your goals for the day, then you are running around with a mind that has no direction. This is a vicious cycle. We all have directions we follow in our lives for various things such as the way we do our jobs, how we drive a car and basic survival needs. So isn't it silly to say we don't have time? We don't have five little minutes to direct our minds and control our thoughts?

I was amazed at the transformation and well-being my life adhered to by magically living in the moment. I started using these steps of quieting the mind and listening with both ears to change my body weight. I had been overweight for the past three years. I tried every diet I could and was working out like a mad woman, to no avail. My weight remained the same. I would hate getting dressed because I had so many different sizes of clothes in my closet that there was no organization. I would go through these clothes and create a bigger mess trying to get myself together. Packing for business trips was very time consuming because I would have to bring so many different pieces of clothing. I decided after many months of devouring every self-help book I could get my hands on that I was going to try this technique of setting goals and controlling my mind to drop my body weight. Thanks to many self-help gurus, including Wayne Dyer and Tony Robbins, I was able to shut my mind down and focus on the process of conscious thinking. Right away, I felt euphoric and started feeling an overwhelming sense of peace. I was able to open my ears, control my mind and drop 50 pounds. I have freed up so much time which was previously spent on getting dressed that I am now able to do much more productive things like yoga, journaling, reading and being a life coach. Making the most of moments in your life will introduce you to a whole new world of opportunities.

I have found my life's purpose as a life coach. I help others grow in all different areas of their lives. I thoroughly believe God has gifted me with the ability to teach. Mentoring and coaching others to find their life's purpose is something I truly enjoy. I have spent the past 24 years as a leader of a dental office and have helped multiple people change their thoughts and create lives of abundance. The Law of Attraction is one of the tools I implement and execute on a daily basis. I am committed to constant and continual growth.

Currently, I am working to raise money for homeless families in my hometown. Multiple hours of my time will be spent helping these fabulous souls get back into the game of life. Giving back to the universe is the best part of this journey. Life is about contribution and I can't think of a better way than guiding others into a life of abundance. Together, we are all supposed to enjoy a life of peace, love and contribution. By consciously choosing your thoughts, you will find a life full of gratitude and abundance.

Lean into your mind, fall into your soul.

Lori Meadows

DON'T DREAM IT, BE IT
Lora Herring

Throughout my college years and into my early 30s, I worked in the hospitality industry. I learned how to provide good service and keep people happy because my income depended on it. I always worked at small establishments owned by individuals where my creativity, individuality and problem-solving skills were highly valued.

Following this, I went to work for a large corporation. I was repeatedly frustrated by the overly-structured, corporate thinking and the inability to consider each client as an individual or to offer them the level of service I had been accustomed to providing. I was not allowed to make judgment calls to decide the appropriate thing to do in an unusual situation. I was forced to stay inside "the box" and follow the rules. I felt the company didn't value me any more than it valued the stapler or the phone. I was just another piece of equipment, a "human resource." I tried to use my sense of humor to have as much fun as possible, but after a few years, I was miserable. The money wasn't important enough to compensate for the lack of pride I felt for not doing a top-quality job. That's just not how things were done and I simply wasn't cut out to be a corporate robot.

I had a friend who would often burst into song in a loud and dramatic fashion. He would sing, "Don't dream it, be it," from a movie. So, I decided it was time to take a big leap. I left many dear friends and moved to Austin, which had a strong energetic draw for me, as I had loved Austin since I was a small child.

I had recurring dreams at this time about going from room to room through houses. Someone suggested I become a real estate agent. This was an "a-ha" moment for me, but working on a commission-only basis was very scary. I was in a new place without the sphere of influence one needs, such as an organization, church, club, etc., in which a group of people knows you. For a time, I let my fears stop me from moving forward and took another corporate job. I guess I had to prove to myself that it wasn't for me.

I struggled at first, but slowly built my real estate business. I knew that I wanted to help people find their dream home and I found myself almost as delighted as my clients when they found the house that was "the one."

It is usually easy for me to recognize what clients want. I guide them through the process of discovering what is most important to them. I am not interested in "selling" people something that doesn't meet their needs. I don't follow all the conventional realtor methods and I don't use the scripts that I've been taught. I tell people the truth, even if it means no money for me. Now, I'm able to work with people I enjoy. Helping others find the right home is like shopping, which is something I love, and I get to see the joy in their eyes when they find the home that's right for them. I use my expertise to give advice and help them to make the right decisions. The purchase of investment property is all about the numbers, but the choice of a home is more about the heart. I am living my dream when what I do makes a difference and I am able to do this in several ways.

As a dog lover, I also offer my clients help in adopting an animal companion if they choose or in making a donation to a shelter or rescue group. I support these groups myself, sometimes making them the beneficiary of fundraisers. It has also been very fulfilling for me to be able to work to find solutions for people in special situations. I don't just take the easy ones, either. I will never forget the client who worked hard to change her life after being raised around gangs, living in poverty and having a husband in prison. Although she and her children lived in a tiny apartment in a rough neighborhood when we met, it was neatly decorated and her children were polite and respectful. My best lender and I found a way to get her into a home for a total cost of $17. She never believed she could have her own home, and she cried. That was more rewarding than earning a big commission could ever be.

I really do have my dream job now! I have met interesting and fun people through being a realtor, and I have a great deal of flexibility in my schedule, which allows me ample time for being with my wonderful friends, learning new things and meeting like-minded individuals. I also enjoy the Austin music scene, and my passion: salsa dancing. I have the time to be with my aging parents and help them as they need it. Being happy, finding time to do things I enjoy and having my work truly benefit others makes this the life I want. I follow my passions and trust that the money will come—and it does. I am grateful for the gifts I have been given such as family, friends and talents. I wonder what I'll dream next!

Lora Herring

STAYING FOCUSED AND PRODUCTIVE
Tom Hopkins

If you're like most people today, you're focused on making more money, keeping more of what you make and still finding ways to create wonderful memories of time spent with loved ones. A necessary element to happiness is to also achieve a high degree of satisfaction with everything you do. It's what we all want, but few of us accomplish it. We schedule our days and nights so tightly that if we miss something, we feel like failures. We are constantly asking ourselves how many ways we can multi-task. It's as if multi-tasking has become the goal instead of enjoying the fruits of our labors.

In my early real estate sales career, I worked a ridiculous schedule. I was the first one in the office every morning, filling every hour of the day with phone calls, door knocking, attending meetings, canvassing properties, more phone calls and paperwork, then heading home well after dark. For three years straight, the only day I took off was Christmas. I was extremely focused and amazingly productive, but my life was out of balance.

Never having been a good student in school, I quickly learned as an adult to constantly be on the lookout for educational opportunities. When I heard about someone who was very successful, I tried to study his actions so I could improve my own level of success.

One day I heard a story about one of the most successful businessmen in my area and his lifestyle. I wanted to know more, so I contacted his office and asked to take him to lunch. I didn't really expect that he'd do it, but I persisted and eventually he agreed. While waiting for our meal, he asked what I wanted from him. As with many successful people, he received a lot of requests for financial donations, business advice, involvement in new ventures and so on. I told him I wanted to hear how he became so successful, which must have surprised him because he became silent. He then replied, "Tom, I'm going to give you some words that have made all the difference in my life—not just in my career. There'll be days you'll hate me for having shared them. Then, there'll be days when you'll understand their power."

I thought, "Wow, he barely knows me and he's agreeing to give me the keys to his success." I was elated, but I was also young and unprepared. I had neither a pen nor paper to take down these words of wisdom I was convinced would change my life forever. I borrowed his pen, picked up a paper napkin and told him I was ready. Then, he gave me only 12 words. However, these 12 words have made all the difference in my life.

Here they are for you, "I must do the most productive thing possible at every given moment." It's the simplest method I've ever encountered for getting enjoyment from each of the 86,400 seconds we all have in a day. Simple? Yes. Easy? Not always. When you begin contemplating how you use your time (spending it or investing it) based on those 12 words, you are forced into the moment—the now—and begin to set wise priorities. You find you enjoy yourself more and are more balanced and comfortable with your life.

If you will dedicate yourself to living that declaration, you will find that in some "given moments," it's more productive to make phone calls. At other times, it's more productive to watch your children practice or play sports. Other moments call for lying on the beach on a warm, sunny day, savoring the fruits of other productive moments that have helped you earn the income for the rejuvenating beach vacation. However, it doesn't change anything to look at those words once in a while and think, "That's what I'm going to start doing just as soon as I can get myself together." If you really want to achieve, start living by those dozen words now.

Doing so requires only four steps. Imagine, only four steps to all the success you want. Let's get one thing clear at the onset. Doing the most productive thing possible means just that—the most productive thing.

It doesn't mean looking busy, getting by or putting things off. It means doing the most productive thing possible at that given moment, no matter how distasteful, hard or worrisome the thing might be.

This often means working through a knotty problem, facing up to an unpleasant task, or heading into a likely rejection. It means shooting for the top when you know you should, even if you are afraid. It means preparing when you need to prepare and doing when you need to do. That's why I say it isn't easy and why so few people follow it. Anyone can do it; you just have to want to. Here's how. Consciously repeat these four steps to yourself until they become second nature.

1. Tell yourself, "I must do the most productive thing possible at every given moment."
2. Decide what the most productive thing is.
3. Do it.
4. When you've pushed as far forward as you can right now, go back to the first step and start over.

Sometimes the most productive thing you can do at any given moment is to sit down with your favorite person and spend an hour watching the sun go down. Sometimes the most productive thing possible will be exercising, sleeping or taking that well-deserved vacation. And, very often, the most productive thing you can do will be the last thing you want to do. The line between winners and losers cuts sharpest at this precise point.

We live moment by moment, not year by year. Do the most productive thing you can think of with each and every moment and your future will be secured. Do that all day, every working day and your progress will soon astound everyone who knows you. More importantly, you'll be astounded, delighted and justifiably proud of yourself.

Within minutes of dedicating yourself to this plan and putting it to work, you'll notice a difference. Within hours of making this plan yours and beginning to do the most productive thing possible with every given moment, you'll project a new aura of confidence and capability. Within days, people near you will sense the difference and begin upgrading their opinions about your abilities and prospects. Within weeks, you'll be reaping substantial rewards from your new willingness to pay the price of success. Within months, you'll be living on a higher level than you now believe you can achieve in so short a time.

Since it creates a dramatic change after only a few days, imagine what the total cumulative result will be after you have lived by this credo for several years. I can tell you what will happen. It will revolutionize your life. It will send your accomplishments, happiness and career soaring. All this will fall into place if you'll apply it moment after moment, hour after hour, day after day. How do I know it will? Because that's what it did—and is still doing—for me.

Tom Hopkins

AND NOW...LIVING MOMENT BY MOMENT
Kornelia Rassias

I can tell you all about living unhappily and miserably. Actually, I believe I perfected it and brought it to a whole new level. I had become very, very good at it. After years of practice, I became sick and tired. You know the feeling! Most likely, you attended one of my numerous pity parties since I invited everybody.

I can tell anyone about living happily and in bliss. Actually, I believe I am perfecting it and bringing it to whole new level! I am becoming very, very good at it. After a short period of practice, I am ecstatic to know how to create my reality! I hope you will attend my party. I am inviting everyone.

So which version would you like to read about?

In my unhappy version of living, I felt like life was a game that I didn't know the rules to. I began to ask questions and almost immediately received answers. For the longest time I had asked, "*Who* am I?" I know who I am! I am aware of my name, gender, profession and all the roles I am playing. Accepting that everything is energy—including myself—finally led me to the question I had never asked before: "*What* am I?" I am this amazing, divine energy expressing itself in form. I am *what* in *who* form. I also was completely unaware of the communication going on between *what* I am and *who* I am.

One afternoon, my friend and her young daughter came for a visit. As I pre-pared drinks, the little girl looked at me and asked, "Who are you talking to?"

"Nobody," I replied. "I am talking to myself."

She just stood there, looking intensely at and around me. "Oooh, I am sorry," she said, and tiptoed away with reverence. Her reaction got my attention since she had no problem interrupting the conversations between her mother and me. In my mind, I repeated the conversation and ended up with the same question: "Who am I talking to when I am talking to myself?" My initial answer was "nobody." If I am talking to nobody, then the question has to change to: "What am I talking to?" "What" am I talking to refers to the divine energy field that I call "self." All day long, we are giving out or listening to advice on how to interact with "self:"

Love your self.
Respect your self.
Trust your self.
Listen to your self.
Give of your self.
Know your self.
I can see my self in you.

The list goes on and on.

I began to comprehend the dynamics between my *self*—the divine energy—my *ego*, my beliefs, and my reality, the mirror of my beliefs and thoughts and my experiences. Once I understood my reality is a reflection of the interaction between *self* and *ego*, life became amazing.

I wake up around 5 a.m. To be in a body that allows me to feel, taste, see, hear, smell and interact is fantastic. It is definitely a reason to celebrate. Outside it is still dark and very quiet. The air is packed with anticipation. It seems everything, including me, is holding its breath. Then the sun comes up. The celebration begins. A whole new day full of experiences I have created loaded with miracles is ahead of me. I can't help but join those birds in their jubilation!

It is around 5:30 a.m. I already had two parties and I didn't have to arrange anything! No catering service was required and no band had to be hired! I just made the choice to acknowledge and be aware of this amazing energy field and to be in awe of the endless forms and expressions it takes. Filled with gratitude, I go inside to have a shower. A turn of a knob sets the preferred temperature. Thanks to my body, I can feel the warm water caressing my skin. Some drops bounce off like an invitation to play. Consciously, I am interacting with this energy field expressed as water. Guess what—more joy!

Having breakfast is another delightful experience. Not only do I have food and drink, I can also be like a kid in a candy store. I have choices. Mango or orange juice; toast or eggs? Divine energy expressed in the form of mango juice! No wonder it tastes heavenly!

It is 7 a.m. I am ready to gain clear focus and create my experiences. I will be giving another seminar soon. I choose to simplify explanations and enhance visual effects. Shopping is another choice. I make my list. Making phone calls is next. In my mind, I clarify the purpose for the calls. Of course, I have to go swimming.

During meditation, my brain activity slows down and enables me to be alert and focused. I begin to visualize my choices. I feel the happiness those choices allow me to experience. My body tingles. I am excited and extremely grateful. It only took six steps! Clarify my choices, meditate, visualize with clear focus, feel the emotion, act accordingly and recognize the experience.

I am now capable of interacting with people by first acknowledging *what* they are—divine energy—followed by *who* they are—divine energy expressed into a form reflecting my thought processes. The phone rings. My friend, Mary, is asking me questions that require clear answers or she will not stop asking! Once again, I recognize the divine interaction and understand the reason she called was the answer to my choice to simplify explanations for my next seminar. I am thankful and get a kick out of the interaction. Now I go shopping. I will remember to pick up some lip liner. Have you ever counted how many times you are asked, "How can I help you? What can I do for you? Is there anything I can help you with?"

I keep remembering I am interacting with divinity in human form. I am truly in awe. What I see is just incredible. There is an older lady looking stunning in a summer dress, wearing a matching hat and delicate lace gloves. She looks like she stepped out of a movie. How much effort she has put into her appearance for me to see! How incredible is this? When I am thanking her for being so beautiful, she looks at me with a twinkle in her eyes, the biggest smile on her face and thanks me. At the check-out counter I see a container next to the cash register. Naturally, I have to know what it holds. What do you think? Yes! My lip liners! A gentleman is attending the register. I pick three different shades and ask him about the price. He looks at me and smiles: "For you they are free today. Is there anything else I can do for you?" I have to laugh, thank him with all my heart and feel like dancing out of the store. People smile at me and doors are being opened. I can help a mother with her little boy and shopping bags and get another thank you, a big smile and a twinkle in her eyes. As I drive home in my convertible, the wind is playing with my hair, the music is reflecting how I feel as I sing along and I get more smiles from other drivers. As I pull into the driveway, my dogs are there to greet me. It is wonderful to feel their soft coats and to be the object of their affection. Coming home, I am bursting to share all my experiences with my sweetheart. What a wonderful day and we haven't even gone swimming yet!

So, would you like to read the unhappy version now? I am convinced you already have one of your own. I prefer to stay focused on having a happy life and acting alive.

I remember it was my unhappy version that enabled me to wake up and become aware that, while I can't change *what* I am, I can easily change and align *who* I am, just like I fix a program in my computer when it is full of viruses or can't work effectively in harmony with the main programs. It was, and is, only thoughts and beliefs that needed to be adjusted and aligned. It wasn't like I had to go mountain climbing! Yes, you are right. I love the water! I choose to play in the pool now. Once you wake up and understand the mechanics of the system, it is truly easy to live a wonderful life, moment by moment!

Kornelia Rassias

YOUR FUTURE IS NOW!
Lee Beard

Your future is now!" That is easy to say, but it seems that we have a difficult time enjoying the past and looking forward to the future. I must say that one of the best ideas I have ever heard was that you should create your future from your future.

I recently had the privilege to meet with Stedman Graham and experience one of his leadership conferences live. I happened to be sitting on the front row when he illustrated the effect of bringing negative experiences from your past into your present and future. He had a clear glass of water and he poured my orange juice into it. Then he poured that glass of mix into another glass of clear water. The orange juice and water mix diluted and clouded the second glass of water. Had he done that again, he would have continued to taint the next glass of water with the orange juice mix. It was a very vivid demonstration of the lasting effect we cause by diluting our future with tainted memories of the past.

The idea of only allowing the positive and unlimited potential into your present and future can be very encouraging and empowering. I cannot say enough about the benefit of releasing your future possibilities into your life today and for the rest of your days. We seem to be naturally adept at remembering the times when we fell short of our best intentions while ignoring our accomplishments and achievements. We need to permit only the helpful and hopeful resources and possibilities to fill our days and build our tomorrows.

You have the power to make this happen. You have a loving Heavenly Father who cares more for you than you know how to care for yourself, only if you will trust Him. You will be amazed at the liberty that you will experience every day by leaving it all to Him. Try it, you'll like it!

So, the success formula is to leave it all in the hands of your loving Heavenly Father and only allow into your future unlimited possibilities and empowering resources.

Give it a go! Live in the now!

Lee Beard

AUTHOR INDEX

Aila Accad, R.N., M.S.N., the De-Stress Expert, is a dynamic speaker, trainer, author and well-being coach. She is a business owner, Reiki Master and EFT advanced practitioner. Sign up for "De-stress Tips & News" on the Web site and get the Ten Instant De-Stress Tips e-book as a gift. Contact Aila at www.ailaspeaks.com.

LifeQuest International, LLC
Address: 1800 Woodvale Drive
Charleston, WV 25314
Telephone: 304-344-9131
Web site: www.ailaspeaks.com

Author and CEO, OneCoach
The Answer: Grow Any Business, Achieve Financial Freedom, and Live an Extraordinary Life
Telephone: 858-792-1250
Web site www.ReadTheAnswer.com
E-mail: Info@OneCoach.com

Lee is a television producer, advertising executive and business developer. He lives in Arkansas when not traveling as the co-creator of the *Wake Up...Live the Life You Love* book series. Lee is an author featured in more than a dozen motivational and inspirational volumes. He concentrates on bringing the power of the Wake Up network to bear on the challenges of business development. If you've had a "wake up" moment you would like to share, visit wakeupmoment.com to tell your story!

Web site: www.wakeupmoment.com, www.wakeuplive.net, leebeard.com
E-mail: lee@wakeuplive.net

Founder and Spiritual Director
Agape International Spiritual Center

Address: Culver City, CA
Web site: www.agapelive.com

Do you have all the passion and riches that you want in life? Denise can help you get there! She is an award-winning marketing strategist, author, speaker and success coach. She helps people discover and express their passions and create balanced lives they truly love. She also motivates and teaches people in the holistic healing professions (yoga teachers, massage therapists, chiropractors, doctors and dentists) to effectively brand and market their practices and products, sending sales through the roof, all while living a balanced, passionate life. "Passion It Up!" is her motto. Visit the sites for a free gift.

Telephone: 845-429-7983
Web sites: www.PassionUpYourLife.com, www.MarketToRiches.com
E-mail: passionitup@aol.com

As a self-proclaimed eternal student of being, Sam has traveled the globe, learning from out-of-the-box thinkers of the modern era. As a constant advocate for living an inspired life, he has spoken around the world on the topic, "being in the now." Whether he's out at Waimea Bay when the waves are over 40 feet high or simply spreading his words of encouragement, Sam's smile, sense of adventure and views on life are contagious.

Address: 45-553 Koolau View Dr.
Kaneohe, HI 96744
Telephone: 808-216-9165
Web site: www.consciouslycompetent.net
E-mail: holomua2@mac.com

Chris is an endurance athlete who has completed more than 50 marathons, five ultra-marathons and an ironman triathlon (2.4 mile swim, 112 mile bike, 26.2 mile run). He and his wife Arlene have built a successful independent insurance agency over the past 30 years, currently employing more than 35 people.

Address: 333 Route 25A, Suite 150
Rocky Point, NY 11778
Telephone: 631-744-1393
E-mail: chrisdclausen@yahoo.com

Dr. Ruth Diamond graduated with an M.B.B.S. from Sydney in 1953. Since 1954, she has performed an increasing variety of general practice medicine work in New South Wales, including with Aborigines, New Zealand locums for two years, mission vessel home and primitive seasonal work in the South Pacific. She has been in Queensland since 1990, doing general practice work, counseling and writing Words of Wisdom articles for www.chaplain.org.au. Since 1999, she has been doing bioidentical hormone replacement therapy, and since 2005, she has been a cancer support doctor.

Address: P.O. Box 1364
Caboolture, Qld., 4510 Australia
E-mail: joanruthand@hotmail.com

Best-selling author and lecturer.
Wayne is the author of these best-selling books: *Power of Intention, Real Magic, Manifesting Your Destiny* and *Pulling Your Own Strings.*

Sharla Evans enjoys assisting individuals in discovering their eternal light, their authentic self and in reaching their goals personally, professionally and artistically. She is an author, Certified Solution Focused Coach, Inner Journey Guide and Certified Professional Coach. She is author of the *Light Your Candle Inner Journey Book Program*™. To order your Light Your Candle Inner Journey Book Program™ please visit:

Web site: www.Lightyourcandle.com
E-mail: sharlaevans@lightyourcandle.com

Laurie Fitzgerald is a speaker, author and direct selling coach. She is also director of Champion Direct Seller Pty, Ltd.

Address: 19 Cinnamon Court
Redcliffe Qld, Australia 4020
Telephone: 07 3885 2006 Mobile: 0416033722
Web site: www.championdirectseller.com.au
E-mail: laurie@championdirectseller.com.au

Tony specializes in helping teams from Fortune 500 companies, small businesses, government agencies and non-profit organizations achieve breakthrough human innovation through enhanced creativity, strategic thinking, problem solving, management and leadership. Tony helps clients achieve better self-understanding to improve communication and team development through coaching, consulting and workshops.

President, Sixty Sigma, Inc.
John Hancock Tower, 875 North Michigan Avenue, 31st Floor
Chicago, IL 60611
Telephone: 312-794-7768, Fax: 312-794-7801
Web sites: www.SixtySigma.com, 60secondstrategist.com

Benjamin "BC" Green is an accomplished teacher and life coach who believes in miracles in life. He is the creator of Personal Synergetics and is an author, artist and inspirational speaker. Specializing in supporting families of tweens and teens, he has assisted men and women of all ages find balance between their thoughts and emotions, helping them to realize their goals and to live the lives they want.

Personal Synergetics
Telephone: 803-917-9103
Web sites: www.Think-Feel.com, www.oddben.com
E-mail: bcgreen1093@yahoo.com

Sid Grosvenor is a retired Dallas Police Lieutenant, licensed Texas attorney (inactive status), travel writer, Web copywriter, Internet marketer/publisher, retirement consultant, and realtor (Lake Chapala Real Estate de C.V.). He is also the host of www.ChapalaClub.com, an interactive E-Zine dedicated to Lake Chapala, Mexico. Sid and wife, Arcelia, are living their dream at Lake Chapala, Mexico.

> Address: 5802 Bob Bullock C1
> 328 C—99
> Laredo, Texas 78041
> Telephone: 972-635-5290

Madisen is a speaker, inspirational author and life enrichment mentor. She aims to create a world of inspired employees, content co-workers and mentoring managers. She helps people move from loathing, to liking, to loving their jobs by changing their attitudes, behaviors and/or environments. She mentors and encourages others to enrich their lives in the areas of self, health and wealth. Visit her site to subscribe to her free video newsletter.

> Address: 8721 Santa Monica Boulevard, #829
> West Hollywood, CA 90069-4507
> Telephone: 310-594-5138
> Web site: www.MadisenHarper.com
> E-mail: Madisen@MadisenHarper.com

Dr. R. Winn Henderson, #1 best-selling author, has written or co-written 33 books. He also hosts the internationally syndicated radio talk show *Share Your Mission*. If you have a mission and passion you want to pursue, there is no better platform than a radio Internet talk show in which to share it with the world. He can teach you how to get on the air and be broadcasting in 30 days or fewer.

> Telephone: 877-787-3127 (toll-free)
> Web sites: www.theultimatesecrettohappiness.com, www.winnhendersonmd.freelife.com,
> www.winnhendersonmd.com
> E-mail: drhenderson7@mchsi.com

A native Texan, Lora lived in Minnesota for several years before coming to Austin after a particularly bad blizzard. She graduated from Hamline University in St. Paul, MN, with a B.A. and attended graduate school at the University of Minnesota in Minneapolis. She now sells real estate in Austin and enjoys salsa dancing and life in general.

> "Homes in the Key of Life"
> Address: Austin, Texas
> Telephone: 512-626-4848
> E-mail: Lora@KeyOfLifeHomes.com

Linda S. Hines is an internationally-trained, Licensed Professional Counselor in private practice in Lawton Ft. Sill, Oklahoma. Receiving her master's degree from Boston University, Linda began her counseling career in Augsburg, Germany, and has worked in mental health and chemical dependency for more than 24 years. Specializing in trauma recovery, Linda has advanced training in Bioenergetics Analysis (a form of body psychotherapy), Heart-Centered Hypnotherapy and Emotional Transformation Therapy.

Address: Lawton Ft. Sill, Oklahoma 73506-6567
Telephone: 580-248-0844
Web site: www.thehealingjourney.com
E-mail: lindahines@lindahines.com

George is a financial consultant for personal and business finances. He is a Master Sergeant in the U.S. Army, specializing in psychological operations management and also served as a paratrooper in the Air Force for four years in missile maintenance. He has a B.S. in marketing and speaks French and Spanish. He has been married 24 years to his wife, Jandy. They have two sons, Alex and Adam.

Financial Consultant
Hinestrosa Enterprises, LLC
Telephone: 866-893-4487 (business), 910-261-9316 (cell)
Web site: www.hinestrosaenterprises.com
E-mail: george@hinestrosaenterprises.com

Author of the million-plus selling book, *How to Master the Art of Selling*, Tom Hopkins is also one of the builders of sales champions. Over 4 million students worldwide have benefited from his training. Other books by Tom include three of the popular *...for Dummies*™ series. Tom teaches from his own several years of personal experience. His proven-effective selling skills are available via seminars, books, videos and audio CDs.

Address: Tom Hopkins International, Inc.7531 East Second Street,
Scottsdale, Arizona 85251
Telephone: 800-528-0446, 480-949-0786
Web site: www.tomhopkins.com
E-mail: info@tomhopkins.com

Ernie is currently acting and writing for TV and film and is available for speaking and personal appearances. Ernie has performed in various TV shows, movies and plays, including *Taxi, OZ, Ghost Busters, The Hand that Rocks the Cradle, Congo, Miss Congeniality, The Crow* and a variety of others. He has also written two published plays, *Rebellion 369* and *My Kingdom Come*, and is working on others in the near future. His personal representative, Thomas Cushing, can be contacted at Innovative Artist, 310-656-0400, and Ernie can be reached through his Web site.

Web site: www.Ernie-Hudson.com.

Chuck Reynolds is chief performance officer at Excel Group Development, which assists clients in enhancing team and leadership effectiveness. Chuck is known as a passionate and inspiring speaker who enjoys helping others succeed. Visit www.ExcelGroupWorks.com for more information.

Chief Performance Officer
Excel Group Development
Telephone: 1-888-89COACH
E-mail: ForChuck@GrowingCoaches.com

Steven R. Rosen is a native of St. Louis, MO. He has spent the past 16 years in the U.S. Army in locations across the United States, Europe and the Middle East. He remains on active duty and is stationed in Duluth, Minnesota. He has been married to his wife Carren for nearly 10 years and they have two sons named Trevor and Maxwell.

Staff Sergeant, U.S. Army
E-mail: s.r.rosen@lycos.com

As a professional speaker, Connie has presented programs to universities, businesses and educational conferences around the globe. A TV show interviewed over 600 channelers from across the USA to select three for a program during which channelers would help people become more effective in their lives. Connie was selected as one of the three. Her spirit teachers, Paularyo, have provided insight and inspiration to thousands.

"Paularyo" is channeled through Connie Russert, M.S.
Address: San Diego, CA
Telephone: 619-226-0351
Web site: www.ToolsforTransformation.com
E-mail: Connie@ToolsforTransformation.com

Veronica offers the "New Medicine," incorporating a full spectrum of natural and vibrational modalities—sacred geometry, color, light, sound therapy and informational medicine. You can reach her below.

Full Spectrum Energy Medicine
Address: P.O. Box 802
Blue Bell, PA 19422-1802
Telephone: 610-275-3371
Web site: www.fullspectrumenergymedicine.com
E-mail: info@fullspectrumenergymedicine.com

Ed is a forward-thinking entrepreneur and the owner of several successful businesses spanning 30+ years. His business philosophy is to bring out the best in his employees by learning each employee's life goals and then developing a plan to achieve them. He also does customized success consultations with business owners and their employees on goal achievement and getting the most out of life. Ed has served on Dealer Councils for two Fortune 500 Companies and has spoken and held training classes internationally. He has received many awards and was inducted into the ADT Hall of Fame.

Telephone: 505-453-5955
Web site: www.sessanow.com
E-mail: ed@sessanow.com

Creator of *Wake Up...Live the Life You Love.* With more than 12 million stories in print, his message is inspiring an international audience. Steven E has been joined in the book series by such noted speakers as Dr. Wayne W. Dyer®, Brian Tracy, John Assaraf and many more inspirational souls. He is now coaching select individuals on the development of a multimillion-dollar information business with their own message to inspire people around the world.

Web sites: stevene.com, wakeupstore.com/pcc

Mark Stinson is "The Brand Innovator." His clients are in health, science and technology. He conducts branding workshops, training seminars, new product launches, and business development initiatives. Overall, his career in marketing spans some 30 years. Mark and his wife, Jenny, divide their time between homes in Chicago and Boise, Idaho.

STINSON Brand Innovation, Inc.
Address: 3304 N. Lincoln Ave.
Chicago, IL 60657
Web site: www.StinsonBrandInnovation.com
E-mail: Mark@StinsonBrandInnovation.com

Brian Tracy is the most listened-to audio author on personal and business success in the world today. His fast-moving talks and seminars on leadership, sales, managerial effectiveness and business strategy are loaded with powerful, proven ideas and strategies that people can immediately apply to get better results in every area.

Brian Tracy International
Address: 462 Stevens Ave., Suite 202
Solana Beach, CA 92075
Telephone: 858-436-7300
Web site: www.BrianTracy.com
E-mail: BrianTracy@briantracy.com

Paul is a partner in Impact Homes, a residential home builder in South East Queensland, Australia, and manages national and international sales and marketing. Paul combines his passion for productivity and accountability with selling and programming skills to create unique solutions for everyday problems.

> Telephone: +61 422 831 701
> Web site: www.usher.net.au
> E-mail: paul@usher.net.au

She began acting at the age of nine (portraying Oliver in the musical of the same name) and continued to work extensively on the stage, performing in over fifty plays at regional and professional theaters in the Tampa Bay area. Liz has appeared as a regular or recurring character on nine television shows including *CSI, The Tick, Maximum Bob, Brotherly Love* and *All My Children* (for which she was nominated for a Daytime Emmy). Her hobbies are writing (she has sold two potential pilot scripts to studios), scuba diving and running. (Bio information obtained from www.IMDB.com.)

Colleen Walters is an international corporate sales director, speaker, author and corporate direct sales consultant. She also serves as the director of Inspiring Greatness Pty, Ltd.

> Telephone: 617-5519-4892 Mobile: +61401115752
> E-mail: inspiringgreatness@yahoo.com.au

In 2003, Victor Whitmore borrowed money on his credit cards to purchase a small uninhabitable home in a rough part of Tulsa, OK. Three years later, he and his company had built a real estate empire with more than $5 million in net worth. Today, Victor runs the company full-time and is a major player in the multi-family and commercial development real estate world. He is the CEO/Co-Founder, Precision Equity, LLC.

> Address: 5555 E. 47th Pl.
> Tulsa, OK 74135
> Telephone: 918-527-5626
> Web site: www.precisionequity.com
> E-mail: victor@precisionequity.com

As founder of The Aspiration Company, Tony Whittle's style is highly energetic and thought-provoking. He believes in challenging clients with unique testing methods. He'll ask you questions that no one in your life has ever posed—ones you wouldn't have even asked yourself! Next he'll help you find your own path to the answers. Then he'll go to work with you. His simple success principles will make a massive difference.

Member of the International Coaching Federation
Fellow of the Institute of Sales and Marketing Management
The Aspiration Company UK Ltd
Telephone: +44 0845 120 3856, Fax +44 0845 120 3857
E-mail: twhittle@aspirationco.com

RESOURCES

Arielle Ford
www.everythingyoushouldknow.com

Navigating the World of Publishing, Publicity and Building a Platform

The world of publishing, promotion, publicity and speaking can be daunting for even the most sophisticated among us. As someone who has represented some of the biggest names in the business and is the author of seven books, as well as a career book publicist and literary agent, Arielle Ford has had the good fortune to learn every aspect of this world. Nearly everyday she meets someone who wants to break into this world and they always seem to think that becoming a best-selling author is as simple as writing a book and printing it at Kinko's.

Navigating the publishing world is complex and time consuming, but with the right information and a willingness to work hard, breaking into this world is very doable. In her program, *Everything You Should Know About Publishing, Publicity and Building a Platform*, Arielle gives you the straight truth about what agents and publishers are looking for, ways to get publicity before you have a book, as well as:

- Why passion and being on a mission are critical to success
- The importance of "walking your talk" and continuing your own path of personal growth
- Why becoming a best-selling author requires more than just a good book
- Steps to launching yourself you can begin today

About Arielle Ford

For the past twenty-five years, Arielle has worked in nearly every aspect of public relations and marketing. She has helped launch the careers and create best-selling books for Deepak Chopra, Jack Canfield, Mark Victor Hansen, Neale Donald Walsch, don Miguel Ruiz, Gary Zukav, Debbie Ford, and many, many other notable authors.

RESOURCES

Brian Tracy International
462 Stevens Ave., Suite 202
Solana Beach, CA 92075
858-481-2977

Brian Tracy International offers three services: Brian Tracy Online, Brian Tracy University and Brian Tracy Speaking. Brian Tracy Online provides learning programs and educational materials to ensure success in the subjects of entrepreneurship, finance, management, personal development, sales, and time management. You will find an array of programs in CD, DVD and book formats to assist in the development of your personal greatness. Visit the Web site at www.BrianTracy.com or call the customer service representatives at 858-481-2977. They are happy to discuss your personal needs and areas of focus to ensure the perfect learning program is selected.

Brian Tracy University is the perfect choice for students who are ambitious, persistent, self-reliant, disciplined, responsible, focused, committed to continuous learning and growth, as well as determined to increase their income and profits. Once you enroll in Brian Tracy University, Brian will teach you how to increase your sales and income, improve your revenues, cash flow and profits, as well as how to become an excellent manager and leader, while boosting your personal productivity and performance. Brian has successfully helped thousands of people reach their personal and financial goals. Allow Brian Tracy to help you achieve these same goals by enrolling today! To speak with the National Enrollment Director, please call 858-481-2977.

Brian Tracy Speaking offers fast-moving, informative, enjoyable and entertaining presentations. Brian has a wonderful ability to customize each talk for his particular audience. He presents a series of great ideas and strategies with a rare combination of fact, humor, insights and practical concepts that audience members can apply immediately to get better results. To book a speaking event, please call Victor Risling at 858-481-2977.

RESOURCES

Tom Hopkins International, Inc.
800-528-0446
www.tomhopkins.com

Tom Hopkins International is the business of Tom Hopkins, North America's #1 sales trainer.

The purpose of the company is to provide the finest selling skills training available in various formats: seminars, audio recordings, books and videos.

The company is dedicated to helping those who have chosen a career in selling as their profession to learn how to serve their clients most effectively. This includes methods for finding new business, setting appointments, building rapport, qualifying, presenting products and services, and closing sales.

The company's free, monthly E-newsletter provides you with powerful and proven-effective strategies and tactics to assist you with building your confidence in business and in gaining the trust of potential clients. Subscribe today at www.tomhopkins.com and start improving your skill level immediately!

NOETIC PYRAMID

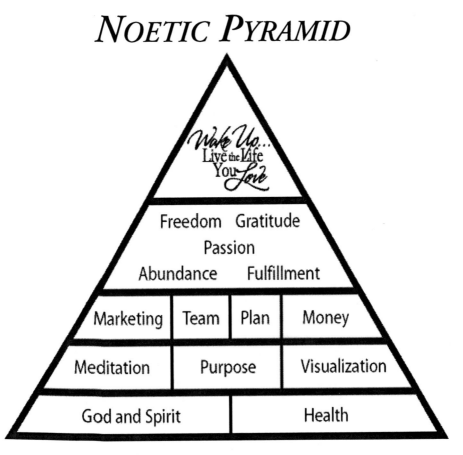

The Noetic (no-EH-tik) Pyramid is a systemic way of looking at the benefits of learning and implementing the attitudes, beliefs and behaviors that must always precede real abundance in life.

NOESIS (no-ë'-sis, noun) [Greek. To perceive] 1. Philosophical: Purely intellectual apprehension. 2. Psychological: Cognition, especially through direct and self-evident knowledge. Noetic (adjective).

There is a way to know; therefore, there is a way to know what to do in life. The answers are not concealed from us, but are available through noesis: a purely intellectual process which gives us sure answers, if only we will look and grasp what we see.

But no one can see—or even look with energy and purpose—unless the mind is clear and the attention is directed. We need a guiding principle that gives us a direction and a foundation.

Building on what they have discovered over years of working with teachers, mentors, motivators, philosophers, psychologists and business leaders, Steven E and Lee Beard have devised the Noetic Pyramid: a structure of beliefs and learning that takes us from the firmest of foundations to the kind of life we can most enjoy; the kind of life which can most benefit those around us; the kind of life that may change the world.

Foundations
With your firm faith in God, you have the proper perspective to process all instructions that you receive. Then, when you give adequate attention to your health, you have a solid foundation to allow you to learn and utilize what we call The 7 Secrets of Living the Life You Love.

Charting the Course
Then we must develop the internal structures of abundance: find your purpose through meditation or prayer, then visualize your desired future. To embark on this process without a firm grounding in belief and without the physical tools to support your mind and spirit, you are almost sure to be disappointed.

Reach Out to Expand the Possibilities
The Pyramid then leads you from a firm foundation to the external techniques of planning, teamwork, marketing and acquiring the necessary money. None of these external elements will be meaningful without the foundational elements, but neither will these essential elements inherently lead to abundance.

Abundance and Gratitude
We must realize the benefits of learning and utilize the internal structure and external techniques to create abundance, freedom, gratitude and

fulfillment so we can truly live the life we love. An abundant life has meaning beyond ourselves, so we must seek to improve the lives of others. When we use our freedom to the benefit of others, when we are thankful for the opportunity to share the blessings of a materially abundant life, then we are fulfilled beyond our ability to imagine.

This is what we want everyone around the world to do: *Wake Up...Live the Life You Love.*

LaVergne, TN USA
12 November 2009
163862LV00004B/46/P